Praise for *Keep Telling Yourself*

"In *Keep Telling Yourself*, Chad Sanschagrin's engaging narratives and actionable tips are designed to help readers overcome self-limiting beliefs and step into a world of endless possibilities. This book is a powerful catalyst for change and a must-read for anyone serious about transforming their life."

—David Meltzer, CEO, Sports 1 Marketing; Speaker; and Author

"Chad pulls from all the best sources, including his own lived experience, to deliver a book that is uniquely useful to help us develop the self-awareness, energy, and self-love that is absolutely a prerequisite for success in any realm. There is no human who won't benefit from devouring this book."

—Shawn D. Nelson, Founder, Lovesac, and Author, *Let Me Save You 25 Years*

"There's a lot of advice out there for creating the life you want, but none of it will yield results for you like *Keep Telling Yourself*. I can't imagine anyone better to have in my corner than Chad Sanschagrin."

—Katie Hoff, 2x Olympian, 3x Olympic Medalist, and 8x World Champion Competitive Swimmer

"*Keep Telling Yourself* is a game-changer. This insightful approach to mindset and personal growth provides a clear road map to living a life of abundance. Highly recommended!"

—Todd Anderson, Founder, Dream Recovery and Synergy Dryland; Sleep and Performance Coach; and Speaker

"A treasure trove of wisdom and inspiration. Through relatable stories and practical advice, Chad guides readers on a journey to discovering their potential and creating a life of abundance. This book is an indispensable handbook for those who want to harness the power of positive thinking and achieve extraordinary results."

—Claude Silver, Chief Heart Officer, VaynerX, and Speaker

KEEP TELLING YOURSELF

KEEP
TELLING
YOURSELF

KEEP TELLING YOURSELF

Shift Your Story
and Create a Life of Abundance

CHAD SANSCHAGRIN

Matt Holt Books
An Imprint of BenBella Books, Inc.
Dallas, TX

Matt Holt is an imprint of BenBella Books, Inc.
10440 N. Central Expressway
Suite 800
Dallas, TX 75231
benbellabooks.com
Send feedback to feedback@benbellabooks.com

BenBella and *Matt Holt* are federally registered trademarks.

Printed in the United States of America
10 9 8 7 6 5 4 3 2 1

Library of Congress Control Number: 2024025035
ISBN 9781637746486 (hardcover)
ISBN 9781637746493 (electronic)

Copyediting by Scott Calamar
Proofreading by Ashley Casteel and Cape Cod Compositors, Inc.
Text design and composition by PerfecType, Nashville, TN
Cover design by Brigid Pearson
Printed by Lake Book Manufacturing

Special discounts for bulk sales are available. Please contact bulkorders@benbellabooks.com.

CONTENTS

CONTENTS

AUTHOR'S NOTE

This book was written to provide helpful guidance and encouragement. The events, places, and conversations have been re-created
from the author's memory of real-world situations. Some names
and identifying details of the people whose stories are shared here
have been slightly changed to protect their privacy.

ACKNOWLEDGMENTS

To my SPW Daughters Mackenzie and Madison,

As I pen these words, I am filled with an overwhelming sense of gratitude for the two incredible souls who have brought immeasurable joy and purpose into my life. You are the beating hearts of this narrative, the driving force behind every endeavor, and the embodiment of hope and possibility. It is with boundless love and unwavering dedication that I dedicate this book to you both, my daughters, my greatest teachers.

To my beloved Kim,

In the tapestry of life, you are the most vibrant thread—the one that weaves through every triumph, every setback, and every moment of self-discovery. Your unwavering belief in me has been the anchor that keeps me grounded, the light that guides me through the darkest of nights. With every word written, every page turned, know that it is your love and support that fuels my passion and purpose. This book is as much yours as it is mine, a testament to the power of love, partnership, and unwavering commitment.

And to all those who have walked alongside me on this journey:

To my employees and fellow CBM members, whose dedication and expertise have shaped my professional path and whose camaraderie has made every challenge surmountable. Your commitment to our mission to contribute to the betterment of every human being we touch never goes unnoticed.

To my clients, whose trust and confidence have been both humbling and inspiring, driving me to continuously strive for excellence. And to my cherished friends, whose unwavering support and encouragement have been the pillars of strength upon which I lean.

This book is a tribute to each of you, a reflection of the collective experiences, triumphs, and challenges that have shaped us into who we are today. As you turn these pages, may you find solace in the power of personal narrative, and may our shared stories serve as beacons of hope and inspiration in your own lives.

With much love and gratitude,
Chad

FOREWORD

*A*nything that Chad does, *I'm betting on him because he doesn't give up.*

Years ago, Chad was at my house for a mastermind event that I held in January. It was a small group, like ten of us, and we spent a few days focusing on growth—every aspect of it. And had we woken up on Sunday, ate some fruit and smoothie bowls, and then said our goodbyes, it'd have been considered a great weekend. But on the last morning, I looked at the frozen hill behind my house and suggested we climb it. Chad's eyes lit up like a kid on Christmas morning.

The hill is no joke; it's so steep it gives other hills a complex. I guess we call that elevation envy. As we began our ascent, everyone struggled, slipping and sliding back down as soon as they made any progress. Chad was no exception. I watched him lose his footing and tumble down repeatedly, each fall more brutal than the last. But he picked himself up every time, spit out the snow and ice he accidentally ate, and started climbing again. He would not give up.

"Come on, we can push past this!" I told the group, but Chad's relentless drive and unwillingness to give up truly set the tone. He didn't complain or hesitate. His focus was firm, his commitment unshakeable. We kept climbing repeatedly, and no matter how many times he fell, Chad's resolve never wavered—ever. By the time we finally reached the top, it was clear that he was built differently; his refusal to give up is what sets him apart.

So, when Chad asked me to write the foreword for his book, I was like, hell yeah. As someone who loves pushing boundaries and going a few extra miles after the tank hits empty, I knew I would connect with his message and the transformative power of his journey. And I was right: this book is more than a collection of ideas; it's a blueprint for unlocking potential.

I met Chad when he cold-called me after reading my book *Living with a SEAL*. Actually, it was a cold email, but you get the point. Intrigued by the story, he googled me and discovered I was starting a small group called BYLR (Build Your Life Resume). Chad joined the second cohort, and he was all in from the start. He never missed a call, always engaged, and frequently asked thought-provoking questions that benefited the whole group. His dedication and enthusiasm were evident from the get-go, and that's how our relationship began eight years ago.

Over time, Chad has become more than a participant in my programs; he's become a friend. I've seen him grow, personally and professionally, and his drive and motivation are qualities I deeply admire. When Chad sets a goal, I set my watch because it's just a matter of time until he's been successful.

Much like his life approach, Chad's book is filled with wisdom and insights. Whether you're an executive, an entrepreneur, or simply looking to make a positive change, this book offers a way to get there. One aspect of the book that really struck me is Chad's emphasis on storytelling. He believes that the stories we tell ourselves shape our reality, and he challenges us to rewrite our narratives in a way that empowers and motivates us. This concept aligns perfectly with my own belief in the power of mindset and the stories we live by. It's a reminder that we're the authors of our lives, and we can change the plot at any moment.

Are you ready to change your plot? If so, keep reading; he can help you write your future.

I learned from Chad that if you repeatedly tell yourself tales of victimhood, you will continue to live a life marked by it. Conversely, if you tell yourself stories of victory, you will lead a victorious life. I mean, who wouldn't want that? It's crucial to be mindful of this, much like the principle in *The Four Agreements* that emphasizes being impeccable with your word. We must be impeccable with the stories we tell ourselves. It's about mastering the art of storytelling, not just for others but, more importantly, for ourselves. I couldn't have said it better myself.

And I'm pretty confident you'll find yourself nodding along as you read this book, maybe taking notes, and feeling a surge of energy to get shit done. His authenticity shines through every page, making connecting with his message and applying it to your own life easy. Hey, if you can write your own story, wouldn't you want to know the best way to do it? Keep reading!

Jesse Itzler
American Entrepreneur and Author, *Living with a SEAL* and *Living with the Monks*

INTRODUCTION

What's the Story You Keep Telling Yourself?

One of the greatest acts of trust we can offer one another comes down to influence. In granting it, we offer up our time, energy, and open minds. None of us does that lightly. As a speaker and executive coach, whenever I arrive at a corporate office or event, conference, or retreat, I stop, survey the building where I've been invited to have influence, and remind myself: *This is sacred ground.*

Trust has to be earned, every time.

In those moments, I am a version of my best self: eager, ethical, and determined to contribute to the well-being of each person I cross paths with over the course of the day. In that scenario, I'm a self-made man with a little wisdom and a lot of heart, a deep commitment to betterment, and a skill set that'll be valued when I pin on the microphone or take my seat at the table.

The thing is, there's another part of me that's always along for the ride, too—the critic. As I roll up to those very same events, the critic scans the parking lot, takes in an ivy-covered portico or a luxury car or a guy in a thousand-dollar suit, and whispers: *You don't belong here. Your good life sits on sand. You were selfish and unlovable at the start, and before long you'll be back there again.*

Yeah, the critic is one malicious SOB.

I'm sure you have one, too. Maybe it whispers that some past mistake invalidates you. Or that you're a heartbeat away from being exposed as too simple or too smug, too weak or too willful, too selfish or too set in your ways.

Or maybe it tells you that you're past your peak, and it's all downhill from here.

At times, my critic even stoops to hissing that I'm too tall or too old or too bald. It can feel like I've got a petty, childish nemesis riding around in my soul.

The critic tends to spin stories that have just enough truth to poke at old wounds. Maybe reminding you that you came from nothing. Maybe zeroing in on that relationship you just couldn't make work. Maybe mocking your lack of education or experience. Maybe suggesting you got where you are because of connections instead of dedication and perspiration.

We all have our soft spots, and our inner critic knows how to hit where it hurts.

This isn't a matter of imposter syndrome. It's part of the human condition—or at least it's part of any path to growth or excellence. As author Hermann Hesse once wrote, "One who never doubts will never truly believe."

The critic is the doubt, and there's no way to evade its stories if you want to move ahead. You have to deal with them—not just once, but all the time.

Each time I arrive at one of those speaking engagements, I know I'm faced with two stories and a choice.

I *choose* to be the sacred-ground guy. I choose to contribute, choose to care, choose to hone my skills, *choose* to be grateful.

I choose that story for my life. And you choose the story of yours, too.

I didn't always know this was a possibility. In fact, I never considered the power of choosing and owning a narrative until I was forced to acknowledge that the one I'd been telling myself for decades was a fabrication. It was a bunch of memories and feelings that my four-year-old self cobbled together and shaped into what I thought was the Big Story of my life. I'll tell you the whole tragic tale in chapter 2, but the gist of it? That I was unwanted. That I was inferior. That I was a victim. That I had every reason to be an angry and bitter underperformer whenever that suited me.

The things you keep telling yourself have a way of starting to feel inevitable and true, and I could have continued living within the confines of that story for the rest of my life. But one night, on a date, as I looked across the table at a woman who was intelligent and animated and beautiful, who knew what she wanted and how she intended to make it happen, time stopped—and for the first time I considered the narrative I'd been living with and asked: *Is this really all you are? Could you be better?*

After that rare moment of clarity with the woman who would eventually become my wife, I started to feel like the story I'd used to inform my decisions and actions for as long as I could remember was less relevant. If I stood it up next to the man I wanted to be, it was too small, too simple, too focused on other people, too much about what had happened *to* me and not enough about what I was *doing* and was going to do.

I started thinking I could author a different story, write a new program, *shift* the entire narrative I'd been telling myself to something new. Something better.

SHIFT is a word that's come to have layers of meaning for me. As a leadership coach and speaker, I use it as an acronym:

See
How
I
Find
Truth.

The emotional jolt of that meeting helped me see a truth I'd been missing—the fact that I have a great deal of ownership over the direction of my life. It allowed me to begin creating a different narrative—one that was a far better fit for the man I wanted to become. That narrative was full of SHIFTs. It went something like this:

> ❯ I was a terrible student, but when I finally started to learn, I couldn't get enough.
> ❯ I didn't go to college, but I busted my ass to work my way from the professional bottom—washing dishes and sorting dirty laundry—all the way to running the multimillion-dollar company I own today.
> ❯ I grew up without a dad, but I choose to relish every moment of raising my own children.

> I missed out on my first shot at true love, but because of that I never take a day for granted with my brilliant, beautiful wife (who graciously gave me a second chance).

> My life and my résumé are littered with failure, but the heart of my story is in the ways I choose to better myself.

Since I've been living *that* story, I'm grateful for everything I've done and been. And I trust the version of me who lies ahead will surpass the one I leave behind. The critic brings the doubt; I choose the sacred ground. Repeat. Repeat. Repeat.

In my work as a coach, I get to spend my days helping other people recognize the power of their narratives. Our collective stories were the inspiration for this book. In each of the chapters to come, I'll tell you something about myself and my narrative, then ask you to look at the elements of your own story. We'll break them down and ask where they came from. We'll figure out if they align with what matters most to you. We'll look at what it takes to get to SHIFT moments, and we'll actively shape the themes and stakes, structures, characters, and payoffs of your life's story.

By the end of this process, I hope you'll be well armed to face the critic and the doubt. You'll be ready to *choose* the story you want to tell and step into the starring role.

After more than a decade of seeing the power of story in action every day, I believe this is a process that will lift us up, bring us together, and help us become better leaders, partners, and parents.

So, what's the story you keep telling yourself?

THE CANNONBALL BOOK CLUB

My highest hope is that readers of this book will experience their own SHIFT—finding a truth that leads to new levels of personal fulfillment. Maybe that means gaining confidence. Maybe it means becoming a better leader. Maybe it means deepening an important relationship (or moving away from one that isn't serving you). Whatever your path, whatever your truth, I'd love for my book to be one on your shelf of titles that encourage, inform, and empower you.

These days, my own shelf of influential titles stretches beyond the bounds of my office, desk, nightstand, and coffee table. It extends to the car, the floor, and the giant (but thankfully not space-hogging) stack of e-books that live in my phone. I believe there's magic in all of them, and sometimes I can't believe I waited so long to experience that unique kind of magic for myself.

These books are a natural extension of my obsession with the power of story. They feed imagination and intellect, open doors we didn't even know were there, and make it blessedly easy to revisit words that resonate with us again and again. I love how every book I read inspires me to consider: *What am I supposed to be learning from this?* And: *What do I want to know next?*

I'll never forget, for example, the first time I read Khaled Hosseini's *The Kite Runner*. The story played out for me like a living experience. I could see the plot unfolding, feel the family's struggle, experience Amir's pain. I got so emotionally invested in the characters that I could not put it down. After I closed the cover, I burrowed into learning more—reading about the author, about whether there was truth in the story, about the history of oppression in a country halfway around the world, and about the refugee experience.

Before I embraced the infinite possibilities in books, I was never like that. I can't remember ever wanting to learn *more* about anything that wasn't right in front of me. I wasn't curious, and because of that I wasn't rewarded with knowledge. Imagine my shock at realizing books are nothing like the sitcoms that were my only comparison—you don't just get in and get out in twenty-two minutes. You carry those words on your soul.

I guess that's why I incorporate books into so much of my coaching practice, and why I've run out of places to put all my favorite titles. As a love note to those books and an acknowledgment of their power, I've included a Cannonball Book Club recommendation (occasionally two) for each of the chapters to follow. I hope you'll share your own recommendations and books that have changed your life with the Keep Telling Yourself community at www.KeepTellingYourself.com.

1

THAT OLD SNAPSHOT

Small stories loom large.

What's your gut-punch photo?

Ever look at an old snapshot and recognize not just the person and place but also the entire emotional landscape of the moment? It's like being transported to the past, to a time when you lived with a different set of experiences, beliefs, and expectations. But when you see that old picture now, you know what happens next—who hit the game-winning run; who stayed together and who drifted apart; even who lived and who died. It's that comparison of what the moment was and how life moved on from it that gives our old photos their emotional weight.

I've got one picture that carries this heaviness more than any other in my life. (Truly—if you want to see a big man cry, just put it in front of me.) It's a shot of my Little League team from when I was ten years old. If you saw it lying around, you'd find it unremarkable—just a bunch of kids in their green jerseys, before or after a game. You might guess it was a happy moment. I mean, childhood baseball? Boyhood pals? Summer and sunshine?

But for me, every glimpse of that photo is a gut punch. That version of me—the tall kid who doesn't have his hat, whose shoulders are hunched, who is glowering at the camera while everybody else grins—that boy was utterly miserable. And not just that day. Truth is, back then, unhappiness was my default. Showing up half-prepared was my style. Seeing intrusion and irritation everywhere was my worldview. I was a child who couldn't grasp contentment, even when it was within reach, who couldn't get comfortable in his family, in his peer group, or even in his own skin. And I was habituated to thinking all the negativity in my life was everybody else's fault.

As a boy, and later as a young man, I played off that unhappiness with self-deprecating comments, with getting in trouble, with barely passing grades, with being a joker. But every jab I took at the world left an internal bruise. A few years ago, when I came across the Little League picture, one of just a few that exist from my childhood, it stopped me in my tracks—because it's the only one I've ever seen that accurately depicts the way I felt inside during that part of my life.

The saddest thing about that picture is that when I look at it now, I know that kid has about fifteen years of poor choices, bad feelings, and strained relationships ahead. That's how long it's going to take before he figures out he's worthy of more; before he starts taking steps toward a life of love and laughter, accomplishment and leadership.

Along the way, between the years that photo was taken and the ones when I began to come into my own, every once in a while I'd get the sense that I was missing something. Like the day I stood behind the partition of a conference room at the Baltimore hotel where I was a houseman, listening to a speaker bring an audience to their feet, wondering what it must be like to be invited to an event like that.

Or the afternoon I was clearing tables from a luncheon and found a copy of Gabriel García Márquez's *One Hundred Years of Solitude* beside a place setting. It was battered and dog-eared, the binding pulling apart, and I wondered how it might feel to care so much about a book that you could wear it out. I should've turned it in at the lost and found, but instead I brought it home and set it on my windowsill. I didn't actually *read* it—that would have been far outside my lifestyle back then—but I felt compelled to hang on to it.

And once in a while, on a night out with my buddies, I'd set down my beer and look at my hands or the bar or the neon signs behind it and think, *Is this it?* Because sometimes it didn't feel like enough.

In those moments, I moved into a particular kind of suffering— the ache you feel when you suspect you are capable of more and better, but you keep settling for less. You keep telling yourself to get used to this imbalance and hoping it'll go away. Or you keep telling yourself to find a little joy in the moment and forget about the future. Or you keep telling yourself that whatever success you have in one aspect of your life makes up for the failings in another.

You keep telling yourself all of this, but that uneasy feeling persists.

It's a kind of suffering most of us experience at one time or another, whether it comes in the form of boredom or jealousy, depression or frustration, or just a vague longing. It bubbles up when we tolerate people talking down to us, or when we fall into the habit of being brutally hard on ourselves. It rankles when employers (or employees) manipulate us, or when family members (even ones we adore) steal our time and energy. It manifests as tension or stress or even physical aches and pains when we choose to hold or lower the bar on what we believe we're worthy of having in our lives.

Since I started my executive coaching company, I've worked with thousands of clients, and I rarely meet a single one who doesn't know this feeling—even though many of these people appear to have it all. They're CEOs and VPs, sales executives and managers, team leaders and valued contributors. But even though most didn't fritter away fifteen years of their lives as I did, they know the suffering of stagnation, frustration, and doubt.

I bet you've got a gut-punch photo, too. An image from the distant or recent past that pushes your buttons and tees up your life's regrets. It encapsulates your own unique brand of suffering—of knowing that you are settling for less than you can do or be. Consider a few examples:

> A powerful CEO whose photo is of a past work team—one he knows he tore apart by being disrespectful and unyielding, managing them the only way he thought he could be effective.

> A top sales exec whose photo is from a professional conference. It's just a picture of a man at a podium, but he

knows it was taken the day his wife called and said she'd had all she could take of being the last priority in his life.

> An amazing director of marketing whose photo is with a group of friends at the beach. He's standing in the back, head down, holding his breath, consumed by insecurities rooted in being out of shape.

> A kick-ass VP whose photo is of her family on a day when she felt so completely overwhelmed by the demands of her life that she was seething behind her smile. All she could think about that day was the time alone she'd be able to "steal" later that night.

> An accomplished entrepreneur whose photo ran in the local paper alongside a profile of her work. She's built a multimillion-dollar company, but when she sees her own face staring back from the page, she *still* doesn't feel worthy of the respect of her business community.

> A hardworking hotel crew member like I was, whose photo is taken on the back side of a partition as he waits to reset a conference room, all the while thinking, *I could do what they do over there. I could earn a seat at that table.* But he doesn't know where to start, so he just keeps up the status quo, going nowhere.

See what I mean? Good people. Hardworking people. Successful and amazing people. On many levels they are absolutely crushing it. But they all have enough insight to know they are capable of being *better.* One could be a strong, compassionate leader. One could revitalize a faltering relationship. One could rediscover good health and body positivity. One could figure out how to slow down a life that feels like a circus of spinning plates and tightrope walks. One could reach a place in her life where she feels satisfied with all she's done instead of consumed by what she hasn't. One could take the first step toward bettering his position.

We all have things we'd say to that past version of ourselves, regardless of whether your picture is from twenty years ago or just yesterday. Maybe something as small and simple as: *Tell your wife you love her today.* Or: *Go for a walk; you'll feel better.* Or: *Nobody is allowed to treat you that way.* Or: *You're right, you can do more—so get started.*

If I could go back and talk with my childhood self—that sad, sullen kid in the Little League uniform—I'd tell him that the biggest tool he has at his disposal is knowing that whatever he keeps telling himself becomes his truth. I'd tell him that all the things he's been endlessly whispering—that he's not loved, that he's dumb, that he's awkward looking, that the world is out to get him—those are stories he can change.

I'd take him by the shoulders, get low so I could look him in the eyes, and say, "You keep telling yourself you're not good enough—but you are just as capable as anyone on that ball field, or in your class, or in your house. You keep telling yourself you're not loved—but there are people who are absolutely devoted to you. You keep telling yourself you're angry and unhappy, but you have a choice. Tell a different story. See what you can do and what you can be."

If I could go back and talk with my childhood self—that sad, sullen kid in the Little League uniform—I'd tell him that the biggest tool he has at his disposal is knowing that whatever he keeps telling himself becomes his truth.

The catch, of course, is that I can't go back. We don't get to hash things out with our past selves. So I do the next best thing: I keep that photo on my desk. I look at that miserable kid. Every. Single. Day. (And yeah, most days he still gets me choked up.) Sometimes I shake my head at what a dumbass he was. Sometimes I have to brace against a wave of frustration at how he could have done things differently. *Always* I appreciate him and what he went through.

And then I shift my attention to the other photos I keep close— my beautiful family grinning into a webcam, my phenomenal professional team posing up a storm under the boughs of a massive live oak, my ear-to-ear smile at six o'clock one Texas morning when dozens of my coaching clients showed up to accompany me on my morning run. If I need more, I skim through a few of the 67,262 photos I have on my phone. (No, that number's not a typo, and by the time you read this there will undoubtedly be more.) Every picture is a reminder of something I did, something I love, something I am learning, or something to which I aspire.

And then there's my empty frame: the antithesis of the grumpy kid with the terrible attitude and the sorrowful eyes. It represents my intention—my commitment—to getting better and gathering cannonball moments for decades to come.

What's a cannonball moment? It's an instant when you glimpse the significance of everything that's come before and gain clarity about how you move ahead. It can be as small as a perfect morning run or as monumental as holding your baby for the first time. It's a moment when you don't have to wonder why you bother with everything you do, or worry about what comes next—because it's all right there, crystal clear, encapsulated in that sliver of time.

When you're working toward those moments, you can put your gut-punch snapshot in perspective—regardless of whether it shows how far you've come or how far you have to go.

A cannonball moment can be as small as a perfect morning run or as monumental as holding your baby for the first time.

It's a moment when you don't have to wonder why you bother with everything you do, or worry about what comes next—because it's all right there, crystal clear, encapsulated in that sliver of time.

BETTERMENT OVER ACHIEVEMENT

Taking authority over your story typically leads to an initial burst of great things—big attitude, new energy, and an amazing sense of relief that you're *finally* doing something to address the gap between what you're capable of and what you've chosen to accept so far. It also leads to the setting of a raft of new goals. It's a natural next step.

That said, when I work with a coaching client who reaches this turning point and says, "I'm going to win X award . . ." or "I'm going climb X mountain . . ." or "I'm going to make X amount of money . . . *and then I'll be satisfied*," I know they're going to meet frustration down the line. Don't get me wrong; all of those goals are completely legitimate, and if they get you moving in a positive direction, then they serve a purpose. Whatever it takes to move that needle is the right thing right now.

However, you can save yourself a lot of heartache down the line if you SHIFT your goals from being focused on singular achievements to being focused on betterment.

Why strive to be *better* when you can shoot for being the *best*?

Because one of two things is going to happen if you're driving toward a singular goal. You're going to hit the mark or you're not. If you don't make it—for reasons that have to do with your capacity, your effort, someone else's actions, or even something as abjectly out of your hands as an earthquake or a worldwide pandemic—then you're going to feel like a failure. Worst case, you may even feel like you're right back to where you started in your gut-punch photo.

But if you *do* make it, then you just walk on air for the rest of your life, right?

Sorry, but no.

You might walk on air for a while—I hope so. But then you're either going to set a new limit on what you're capable of or once again settle for less. Either way you're back in suffering mode.

I worked with a nationally renowned investment authority who sees this all the time in dollars and cents. People think, he says, that if they just have a million dollars in the bank, they'll be happy. The ones who never cross that line think staying short of it is keeping them down. But many of the ones who get there immediately go back into that same "if I only had" mode again, only this time they're certain that if they just had two million dollars they'd be happy. Or ten million. Psychologically, they're right back where they started, focused on the gap between where they are and where they think they need to be to feel satisfied.

I've been in this position. I've set huge goals. (*Be the country's top sales rep! Start a company! Run a marathon!*) I've accomplished those goals and still felt a gnawing sense of lack instead of the glowing satisfaction I was chasing. It took some time to recognize that the trouble wasn't that some part of me is always gonna be dissatisfied. It was that I needed to focus on who I wanted to *become* instead of what I wanted to *achieve*.

I had to go back to what this kind of suffering is: knowing you are capable of more and settling for less. And if that's the case, then as long as you are growing—as long as you are getting *better*—you're fine.

Once you decide you're done suffering over the distance between where you are and where you want to be—then it turns out you can be happy to keep moving the goal. When you're focused on betterment instead of achievement, your quest ceases to be about the medal and starts being about who you are becoming as you pursue it. And suddenly life is filled with possibilities, because when you don't hit a milestone, it's not about how you failed or that you can't do it. It's about not being ready yet. Or realizing you don't need that anymore.

And when you do hit that milestone, you feel great about everything you did to get there—and then you look ahead.

You're always thinking: *If I can do this, then maybe I'm capable of a little bit more.*

It comes down to this: You can keep telling yourself that the benchmarks of your life—in your marriage, in your career, in your health, in your relationships—are pass/fail assessments. Or you can tell yourself that your quest is to become better. When it's the latter, you can feel great about what you've accomplished so far, and you can *always* do more. Push a little harder; learn a little more; be more coachable; shift your perspective; surround yourself with great people; cultivate positive energy.

You can always get better.

When I finally embraced this mentality, this story, I still ran marathons. I still built my company. I still tackled challenge after challenge after challenge—but I lost the sense that I would ever hit a wall. Or stand on top of one and realize there was nowhere else to go. That story resonated with everything else I believed and *want to* believe. It rolled seamlessly into my faith, where I trusted that no higher power would create me to be limited. It fit with my devotion to my family, because I could never imagine suggesting to my überaccomplished wife or our strong, smart, amazing daughters that there's some cap on how great they can be. It fit with my commitment to coaching, because I will never be the guy who looks at a client and says, "Well, you did it. That's a wrap. You're set for this lifetime. Head on home and climb into your recliner, my friend."

At some point in our lives we have these SHIFT moments, and we have to decide: Have I settled for this life? Or am I capable of better? Is there a limit to what I can do and be? Or can I *continually* live the life of abundance and love and growth that I deserve?

> *Once you decide you're done suffering over the distance between where you are and where you want to be . . . your quest ceases to be about the medal and starts being about who you are becoming as you pursue it.*

YOU AND YOUR CAPE

Every path to betterment has obstacles. Some of them are resolvable inconveniences—like branches you have to step over. These are issues like misunderstandings, logistical challenges, or coworkers who don't fully appreciate your value. Other obstacles are tougher to cross—the boulders and brick walls on life's path. These are deeper problems: conflicting but equally vital priorities, deep bias toward you or your work, or a fundamental lack of self-esteem.

That last obstacle—the issue of self-esteem—is something no one escapes entirely. We all sometimes grapple with feeling unworthy of success, or love, or respect. It's a slippery problem, because when you doubt yourself, every other obstacle seems to become outsized. Maybe you don't resolve that misunderstanding because your insecurities keep you leaning toward resentment instead of reconciliation. Maybe you think you can't deal with that logistical challenge because you'll never be able to muster the necessary energy, focus, or time. Maybe you let that dismissive colleague get under your skin because, on some level, you think they're right. Every self-deprecating thought is another stone on the pile of obstacles that blocks your way forward.

The truth is, self-love is a strength that can only come from within—and we live in a world that discourages us from cultivating it. A lot of credit goes to those who are humble and self-deprecating—and those can be great signs of your character. But having a deep-down faith in your own worth and capability is equally important.

I was lucky enough to be inspired to think about this while my daughters were still small. I distinctly remember the day when they were four, going on five, doing what they loved most at that age: dancing. We were just hanging around in the family room, me on the couch, and the two of them jumping, skipping, and twirling around the house. Madison came dancing by me and I said, "Madison! I love you!" and then, just as an afterthought, I added, "Do you know why?"

She didn't even break her stride, moving past me and calling out, "Because you're my dad. You have to!"

She giggled, and I grinned, but something about that answer landed wrong. I thought: *That's not it. That's not enough.* I've often thought this was a God-wink moment. It would have been so easy to let it pass and forget it, but instead, I doubled down.

"Madison, I love you! Now really, tell me why."

She danced over my way, grinning and shuffling her feet.

"Um, because I'm awesome?!"

As she said it, she lit up, beaming a big missing-tooth smile.

Mackenzie came dancing my way and didn't even wait to be asked, saying, "You love me because I'm awesome, too!"

I said, "You sure are!" and watched the two of them dance away—innocent, joyful, kinetic, and proud. I felt a wave of love and gratitude. I also recognized that the pride I was seeing was out of the ordinary. How often do we hear people saying great things about themselves, especially with such innocent, honest confidence?

After that day, I made saying, "I love you; tell me why . . ." a part of our routine. When their answers were about outside factors—like "because you're my dad"—I'd ask again, pushing them to think about it. Eventually, they started to say things like "because I'm a good sister," "because I'm kind," "because I'm a good student," and "because I'm a good Christian." Their answers kept evolving, all the way to statements like "because I'm an amazing human being" and "because I am capable of great things."

Over time, affirmations add up, and these girls were training their brains to be confident and resilient. They were knitting together a kind of superhero cape that would offer protection when the world comes down on them—which it inevitably does for all of us.

It is never too late to start working on your cape—on forging self-love and inner confidence. As that part of you gets stronger, hurts and hardships have less power over you. You can make your cape from affirmations, and you can also build it with gratitude. Every time you invite and appreciate the cannonball moments in your life, you're working on and strengthening the almost supernatural protection that comes from believing in your own worth.

The truth is, we all deal with doubt. The critic doesn't ever go away entirely. But we can get stronger and more capable of holding fast against it—of knowing, to the core, that we are worthy of love and respect, success and happiness.

QUESTIONS
TO CONSIDER

At my company, Cannonball Moments, my employees and I often remind ourselves (and our clients) that we believe *the quality of your life is predicated on the questions you ask yourself.* With that in mind, every chapter in this book includes a list of questions to consider. If you take nothing else from these pages, take those. The questions you ask give you the gift of perspective, and your answers will open your eyes to the things that are limiting you and how to move forward.

> What's your gut-punch photograph? It might be an old print from a scrapbook, or a digital file on your phone, or just an image from a memory that stays with you—always pushing your buttons. What do you see in that moment that no one else perceives? Why is it painful for you?

> What do you keep telling yourself about that moment? That it wasn't fair? That it was the first in a series of mistakes? That you're haunted by something you did or didn't do? That it was the pinnacle of your life (so now you're past your peak)? Whatever it is, it's time to put that into the context of where you are now, what you want now, and your ability to move ahead.

> What is your purpose? Simon Sinek wrote the great bestselling book *Find Your Why*—and articulated a premise that's rightly become ingrained throughout today's business culture. It resonates, in part, because we've all been told at one time or another: "Because I said so" or "Just make it happen." We've all experienced that almost visceral reaction to being pushed toward an action or idea when we can't find any internal justification to do so. When you look at your photo, the first tool you need to put that moment in perspective is something bigger to move toward. The *why* of a close-knit, happy family. The *why* of a fulfilling career. The *why* of being able to connect with other people and support their success.

Why do you get out of bed each morning and do what you do?

> What is your path? A lot of people treasure their purpose—but never get around to doing anything with it. I was that guy for a long time—in that phase of suffering when I knew I was meant for more, but I didn't know where to start or what to do to change it. Purpose without a path is just an ornament. But when you have both, you can learn how to move past challenges and conflicts and even the inertia that sometimes feels like the biggest obstacle of all. As the author of your story, you get to set your trajectory. You determine the themes of your life, the energy and voice you project, the stakes of the work you do, and the relationships you build. Every day, you make a thousand small choices that either carry you along that trajectory or pull you away from it. When those choices aren't taking you where you want to go, it's time to make a SHIFT. New truth = new trajectory. How are you moving forward? How are you steadily getting better?

> What is your superpower? What strength do you draw on when you need more? What's the deep-down internal belief system that shores you up when you are challenged? Maybe it's your faith. Or your history of success. Or the fact that you've got an amazing family at home who loves and supports you no matter what. Maybe it's your capacity to stay positive in troubled times. Maybe it's all of those. If you can't instantly put your finger on this, take a few minutes every day to work on this—going over your strengths and saying them out loud. Each time you engage

in this exercise, you'll be constructing the superhero cape that keeps you impervious to negativity and doubt.

> In what area do you want to go all in right now? This is something that changes. I had to go all in on becoming a good partner to become a great dad. I had to go all in on being a good employee before I could step up as an employer. I had to go all in on believing in my own capabilities to make the leap to being an entrepreneur.

At the time of this writing, I'm choosing to go all in on my health. Why? Because I've found that when I put my focus there, it elevates me in every other area of my life. Getting healthy is making me a better husband, a better father, a better coach, and a better friend. So right now, that's my focus. You absolutely do not need to limit yourself to excellence in just one aspect of your life. We're always hearing that you can't have everything, but I don't buy it. I truly believe that each of us is capable of abundant success and fulfillment across the board.

But you do have to start somewhere. What goal pulls you farthest from the pain of your gut-punch photo? What first step can you take right now to move in that direction?

▪ CANNONBALL BOOK CLUB FAVORITE ▪

The Choice: Embrace the Possible

Dr. Edith Eger

CHAD'S NOTE: On principle, I don't believe in comparing struggles. But when you look at what Dr. Eger went through as a Holocaust survivor, and then *she* tells you not to compare—that you should respect each person's suffering as valid and true—there's really nothing left to do but follow her advice. This is a book that will be forever painted on my heart for its unflinching depiction of one woman's hardship and her lifelong refusal to be defined by that struggle.

There is no hierarchy of suffering.
There's nothing that makes my pain worse or better than yours.

2

ORIGIN STORY

Start at the beginning.

Is your story about what happened to you
or about what you are becoming?

Every morning you open your eyes, climb out of bed, and step back into the story of your life. Are you the author? Or are you a passive participant, letting tales that have settled around you define your expectations and limitations?

For many years, my own story started with a little kid who got robbed of a happy childhood. I slipped back into that story every day, letting it frame who I was, how I felt, and what I did.

It began with a happy event. When I was four years old, I woke up to find a child-sized, ride-on Good Humor ice cream truck under the Christmas tree. It even came with a matching uniform—complete with a gold-trimmed, visored hat. *Best. Gift. Ever.* I hopped onto that sweet ride in full uniform and rode up and down and up and down the block, feeling like the king of the world (because the king of the world and the ice cream man were one and the same to me at that age). Sitting on my truck, swinging my chubby little legs to keep it moving, grinning from ear to ear? That was my happy place.

As I drove around, my father would remind me not to leave my truck in the driveway. He said it over and over. But I was little, not a great listener, completely in the moment—and so I left it in the driveway pretty much every day.

Before long, the inevitable happened: My dad backed his car over the ice cream truck and demolished it. After it happened, I was inconsolable.

This little web of story—the pure joy of the toy and the pain I felt when my father wrecked it—is my earliest childhood memory. The next is that a day later my grandfather was at the house with us, and my mom said we were leaving. Moving to Maryland. We got in the car, drove off, and I wouldn't see my father again for decades.

What I took away from the whole experience was this: the greatest toy any kid could ever have was mine—until the ice cream truck killer maliciously ran it over and then disappeared from our lives.

The tale of how I was attacked and abandoned became a key piece of the life story I woke up with every morning. Every time something went wrong in my life, I'd point to this series of events as the root of my troubles. Bad grades. Suspension from school. Quitting one activity after another. All of it tied straight back to this poor, small, unlovable version of me—a child who could provoke his father to so much anger and spite he'd break my favorite toy and then disappear from the family forever.

That story and all the worthlessness it made me feel became my calling card, and with it I was on a flat path to nowhere. Even as I discovered I had a knack for connecting with people and making friends, and even as I stretched out to a burly six foot eight, I saw myself as the same angry, wounded little guy who'd stood in the driveway with the splinters of his childhood at his feet.

Now fast-forward three decades. My paternal grandfather passes away and I go to New York for the funeral. My brother and I walk in and there's my father. My forty-year-old self has been expecting someone *vile*. I'm looking for the man who committed a spiteful act against a child and enraged my mom so completely that she had to get away. I'm looking for the man responsible for us having to start over with basically nothing: a poor, broken, fatherless family.

I'm looking for the kind of guy who ruins your life.

But when he walks up he looks weary. Tentative. Awkward. When he says "Hello" and "Thank you for coming," he sounds just like, well, a normal human being. By this age I've become good at reading people, and I'm completely confused that the vibe I'm getting from this man is calm and sad. I observe him, waiting to see the villain I've been seething about most of my life, but that guy never shows up.

———

When I got home, I called my mother and told her the man I met wasn't anything like what I'd imagined he would be.

"What do you mean?" she asked.

"Well, you know, someone evil. The kind of horrible human being who would run over a toy to teach a four-year-old a lesson."

She paused before she said, "What are you talking about?"

"Mom. *Please*. Don't act like you don't know."

"Chad, I really have no idea what you're talking about."

I reminded her how he purposely drove over that truck, the one thing that mattered to me back then, to punish me. And of course she left him the next day because of it. And the way those events changed my life. Even as I was saying it, I could hear how strange it sounded coming from a full-grown adult; and I wondered, for just a second, why I was still obsessing over events from decades ago. I chalked it up to being a father myself—which makes such an angry act and its fallout even more incomprehensible.

But my mother said, "That's absolutely not what happened. He did run over your truck—after he told you a hundred times not to leave it in the driveway! But he was *devastated*. For weeks afterward he went out almost every day trying to find another one. There was no internet shopping then. He couldn't find it, but he could not have felt worse about what happened to that toy."

On my end of the line, I was deeply confused. My memory was replaying this long-ago event, trying to make sense of what she was saying. It didn't fit with the story of my life. I was still sure I was right, though, because I knew what happened next.

"But that's why you left the next day."

And then my mother gently unraveled what was left of the story, saying, "Honey, there were six months, at least, between those two events."

Talk about a reality check. I grew up holding on to a narrative in which a small child was the object of a world of anger and rejection. It was the story of a victim. Of poor me. Even if I'd remembered everything correctly, I might have internalized the facts into a story of rejection, failure, and anger. But I've had a lot of time to think about this—time to realize my story was full of my choices. Could I have told that story in a way that made me a hero? Or at least a self-respecting kid who got past it? Could I have given my mom the props she deserved by framing my story as one rooted in the heroic efforts of a single mother? Could my story have been about me and my siblings—about how we pulled together and became bonded for life after our parents' split? Could it have been about how the move to Maryland meant that I lost an overwhelmed and immature father but gained a vast support system of aunts, uncles, cousins, and grandparents I could count on to love me and show up for me?

Yes to all of those—and countless other versions of the story of my young life.

Instead I clung to a version that constantly kept me from feeling worthy of respect, or of love, or of excellence.

If this all sounds a little manipulative, a little devious, it's not. I was a small child when that narrative took shape. The story I kept telling myself for years and years fell into place. I didn't plan it, didn't even notice it was happening, and sure as hell didn't realize it was limiting me. I passively let that narrative grow up around me until it felt comfortable and true.

My brother—just one year older—settled into a different story. He was in the exact same situation as me (minus ownership of the ice cream truck). When our lives got shaken up, he looked to our mother instead of our absent father to figure out what he was about. His story? He was the child of a strong, intelligent, loving woman who faced adversity and worked her way out of it. He watched her pull herself up, go to school, raise her family, build a career, and blossom into the beautiful, amazing person we know today. He, too, lost a father, but he adopted a story of strength and capability. In it, he was a great student, the son who did his chores and helped his siblings, and was a success at everything he worked toward. He believed it and he lived it, launching straight from college into a meaningful career—at the same time I was spending my days washing dishes and most nights perched on a barstool.

I'll never fully understand why I chose the other story, but I do know that it wasn't until I took a step back, considered it, fact-checked it, revised it, and chose to *own* it that I was able to get completely free of it. The heaviest baggage I ever put down was hatred toward a father I didn't even know. After that, the story of my childhood gave me strength instead of taking strength away.

And so began my obsession with the power of narrative.

· EVENTS AND ATTITUDES

You don't have to be a child to have this happen to you. We all do it, all the time. Something happens (or doesn't happen), and a story fills in around it, like so much sand. Over time that sand binds together, becoming stone. If we want to free ourselves, we have to chisel our way out of the old stories that don't fit anymore. And let me tell you, when you do it, when you can stretch, breathe deep, and choose how you move forward—that may be the most freeing feeling in the world.

Something happens (or doesn't happen), and a story fills in around it, like so much sand. Over time that sand binds together, becoming stone. If we want to free ourselves, we have to chisel our way out of the old stories . . . And let me tell you, when you do it, when you can stretch, breathe deep, and choose how you move forward—that may be the most freeing feeling in the world.

The event is one factor. Things happened. I saw what my brother saw and he saw what I saw, but we carried those events forward in two entirely different ways. The truth is, it's not the *events* that dictate your life. The *stories* you attach to those events are what lift you up or weigh you down.

Viktor Frankl, the famed Holocaust survivor and author of one of the most influential books of all time, *Man's Search for Meaning*, wrote that the last of human freedoms is "the ability to choose one's attitude in a given set of circumstances." There are over ten million copies of that book in circulation, because Frankl so eloquently shared this universal truth. His circumstances during three years in concentration camps were tragic to the point of being unthinkable, but Frankl refused to let his persecutors define his story. He would write it himself, and in it he would be a survivor. He'd be strong. He'd be wise. He'd be compassionate. He'd be an educator.

In telling his story his way, Frankl became, for millions of readers, a hero of his time. And throughout his career, he brought attention to the quiet power that comes with being able to choose how you react and how you feel in any circumstance.

Which brings us to your story. Did you *choose* it? Do you throw open that book and stride purposefully into it each day? Is it serving you? Or are you just going along with a narrative that settled around you like so much sand?

If you're not certain, then it's time to question it. Of course there are a thousand stories you carry through your life, so you have to pick a starting place. I like to start at the beginning—with that story from childhood you might use to tell a stranger or a first date what you're all about. For me, for a long time, it was the ice cream truck story—told from the perspective of a kid who felt victimized.

Today I tell a story of transformation and freedom.

GREAT EXPECTATIONS

A good litmus test for your "first" story, the one about how you became the adult you are, is whether it sounds like a true *origin* story. Think superhero. Superman rocketing across the galaxy in a spaceship, growing up powerful but hidden in rural Kansas and then choosing to use his strength for good. Spider-Man, going from an insecure, gangly teenager to an incognito crime-fighting force after being bitten by a radioactive spider. Wonder Woman, sculpted from clay by her mother, imbued with superpowers by the gods, raised by a community of strong, powerful women to be fearless and wise—then taking all that power, valor, and honor to the outside world. (Wonder Woman has been a key figure around my house ever since I became a father of two daughters.)

Superhero stories are great models for this process because they're usually about someone who *became* special, *became* relevant, *became* a force for good.

So where did you start, what happened to you, and what did you do with that experience? Whether you're a seventy-year-old executive running a hundred-million-dollar company or a twenty-two-year-old intern making coffee and copies in a mom-and-pop business, you should be able to look back at your beginnings and find an origin story that sets you up for greatness.

My own origin story about a kid who got a raw deal and never got over it was hardly a tale worthy of a superhero. But then I chose to let it evolve into the story of that kid shaking the chip off his shoulder and looking back with gratitude for all the things that *did* go his way. I chose a story in which my losses and mistakes helped shape a man of purpose and strength.

Once I changed my story, my beliefs shifted to match. Instead of believing I was weak or unworthy, I started to understand I was capable and important. As my beliefs shifted, so did my emotions—from a vague feeling of regret and dissatisfaction to a clear sense of enthusiasm and purpose. Driven by those emotions, I changed my behaviors. I took on more, worked harder, applied myself to my career, health, and relationships.

What followed were changes in my results: More love and stability in my home. More success and achievement in my work. Better health. Higher energy. Happier friendships and professional relationships. Every metric of success in my life improved (as well as a lot of facets that cannot be measured).

That's the power of a stronger, more positive origin story in action. Every day I see coaching clients working through their own evolutions. This is a natural order of processes, one you can put to work in your own life at will:

> *Your stories shape your beliefs.*
> *Your beliefs shape your emotions.*
> *Your emotions shape your behaviors.*
> *Your behaviors shape your results.*

THE ALMOST-GOOD-ENOUGH STORY

Maybe your story is just fine as it is, but most people, when they start to ask questions, recognize aspects they'd like to change and improve. After all, most of us—even those who are extremely successful in one area—are failing at something. I'm not suggesting you ought to be great at everything, but I'd love for you to consider whether you've given up on a part of your story that is important to you deep down. Or if maybe you've unintentionally let a failing or shortcoming turn into a feature that helps define you.

Here's an example I see all the time when I coach people who work in sales: They've internalized the idea that those who sell (anything) for a living are somehow smarmy, or predatory, or users. That's not who they want to be, but they've made it part of their story, and they go out there and live it every day—working under the weight of a mantle of shame that they've rolled up into the story of who they are and what they do.

Do you know how many companies would profit, or even exist, without sales? Do you know how many industries would fall apart? Do you know how many people would go without vital goods and services they need to survive and thrive? Having a sales force is *essential*. The idea that selling can't be noble work is ludicrous. And yet there are millions of people in that field right now who are carrying a tinge of shame around about what they do because they've accepted a premise that shorts them.

Another common case: someone who is extremely good at one thing and has settled for a story in which that's all the excellence they can muster. Great salesman, terrible husband. Great mom, terrible employee. Great leader, but she doesn't take care of herself.

What are people telling themselves by buying into these stories that have been told to them—or that they've told themselves?

"These are my limitations."

"That's just how it is."

"It wasn't meant to be."

All too often, these are the statements that let doubt and shame seep into the stories of our lives.

One more example: individuals who define themselves by their mistakes. For a long time, I was one of these people. The topic of shame is pretty personal to me. Over the years, I've carried a lot of it—for always underperforming, for being a ridiculously late bloomer, for having opportunities right in front of me that I didn't bother to take. For a lot of years, the quickest path for me from confidence to self-doubt came in the form of two simple questions I get all the time. I can usually see them coming. I feel someone taking in my feet, my wide hands, and the distance to my big, bald head. And then they ask: *How tall are you?* and *Did you play basketball?*

I warned you they were simple questions. They certainly don't sound like armor-piercing inquiries. Definitely not enough to rattle a grown-ass, accomplished, confident man.

But that's exactly what they did to me, for years. What caused me angst was the underlying finer point in the question: Did you play *college* basketball?

I didn't. Not because I wasn't good enough (that's something I'll never know), but because I was the epitome of a lousy student. I barely made it through high school. I didn't study. I didn't bother doing homework. I didn't even read. I gave zero effort to my high school education, graduating with a 1.6 GPA (and I promise you, that was a gift).

I made endless choices to ignore my own potential, even while my peers were moving forward with theirs.

And because of those facts that I long considered my private shame, I never went to college. What college would have wanted me?

When asked the anxiety-inducing questions, what I heard, what I asked myself each time, was blunt and cruel: *Did you not play because you weren't athletic? Or were you dumb?* I knew I'd always been athletic, and so I always ended up at the other, more damning self-assessment.

After high school, my first job was sorting dirty linen in a hotel. No child ever named that task when asked, "What do you want to do when you grow up?"

I worked hard, proving my value to my bosses, but also to myself. I began a long, slow climb up the corporate ladder, from hourly laborer to service manager to director of operations. I discovered that I excelled in sales and made the leap to selling new homes. From there, I moved on to coaching other sales professionals, and finally to founding my own company.

Somewhere along the way, I started to feel proud of the man I had become instead of pining for the one I might have been. The reality is, if I had gone to college, I'd be living a whole different life. I would never have worked my way up from the bottom of the corporate world. I would never have met and married Kim, the love of my life. We wouldn't have our daughters, who make me proud and grateful every single day.

You don't get to rip out one chapter of your book and have the same ending. Whether you have to answer armor-piercing questions or you just hear them in your head, your choices led you to where you are today. And if there's a facet of your story that keeps you up at night, that niggles at you from time to time, or that makes you feel ashamed, it's time to make peace with it. Figure out how to roll those prickly things from your story into tales of atonement, change, hope, achievement—any narrative that allows you to move forward and on to your next chapter.

Remember, your narrative is always evolving. That's a good thing. But change takes time. When I coach business executives, I work with them every week for a year. And we *constantly* revisit what questions are being asked and what stories are being told.

Think about it: What part of the story you're living right now makes you uncomfortable? What part doesn't align with your aspirations or expectations? How can you make that factor integral to a forward-facing future—one where you and your circumstances are better?

The chapters to come will help you harness each element of your narrative and move it forward.

If there's a facet of your story that keeps you up at night, that niggles at you from time to time, or that makes you feel ashamed, it's time to make peace with it.

Figure out how to roll those prickly things from your story into tales of atonement, change, hope, achievement—any narrative that allows you to move forward and on to your next chapter.

QUESTIONS
TO CONSIDER

> What's your origin story? Where do you come from? What formative events do you consider most key to who you are today? Know that it's up to you to choose which events and actions are the focus of that narrative. You can't change your past, but you can certainly change which moments you believe are most important. Are you focusing on times when you fell down or failed? Or on how you got up, overcame, or carried on?

> What about your story makes you feel empowered? What about it makes you feel weak? A key feature of empowering narratives is that they're not simply about what you *are*; they're about what you *are doing* and *can do*. If you're focusing on what's been done to you or for you, you don't hold the authority in that tale.

> How comfortable have you gotten with your origin story? How certain are you that it's true? I meet people all the time who limit themselves because some invisible boundary or ceiling is part of their story. They believe they can only have X amount of success, or that they're not "destined" for love, or that they could never be physically fit—without ever asking themselves why, or why not.

> Are you satisfied with your story? Are you dissatisfied? Are you stuck? I've had clients describe feeling as though they're living their lives like Jim Carrey's title character in *The Truman Show*, existing on a contrived set that's supposed to simulate a life. Another simply said, "It feels like my days are the same shit, over and over again." Is there a part of your story that's keeping you locked into a negative loop? Bringing change to your life starts with changing your story. What can you SHIFT in your narrative today to nudge yours in a new direction?

> Are *you* at the center of your story? What observations and opinions from parents, teachers, coaches, siblings, or childhood friends have become part of your definition of yourself? When I took a step away from the story I'd been telling about my own childhood, I couldn't believe how much power I'd given to the person who made me feel abandoned. One person walked out of my life, but I lived in the heart of a big, affectionate extended family. Why give all that authority to a man who wasn't even there?

> Is there another story that fits you better or serves you better? One that can help you become a better worker,

business owner, leader, life partner, parent, or friend? Tell it in a way that focuses on *your* actions, your changes, your objectives, and the pieces of your history you treasure.

▪ CANNONBALL BOOK CLUB FAVORITE ▪

Dark Horse: Achieving Success Through the Pursuit of Fulfillment

Todd Rose and Ogi Ogas

CHAD'S NOTE: This is a thoughtful, brilliant book about the fact that there is no straight line to success. Finding the nexus of what you love, what you're good at, and what you can make a living at is a winding path to fulfillment, and Rose and Ogas share great examples of maverick successes who wrote their own stories, embraced their differences, and made life-changing contributions. This is a title I often recommend to my coaching clients (and also to anyone raising kids!).

Stereotype-shattering stars demonstrate that personalized success does not depend on who you know, how much money you have, or what you score on the SAT.

It is not reserved for those perched at the top of the ladder.

By its very nature, personalized success is available to everyone.

3

BECOME THE AUTHOR

You find what you focus on.

What are the themes of your story? The themes of your life?

One of the exercises I often incorporate into my keynote speeches to demonstrate the power of story is arm-strength testing. If you've never seen this done, I encourage you to try it. Despite the name, this is more a test of the strength of your mind, your words, and your energy than it is of any part of your anatomy. On the surface, the premise is simple: When you *feel* weak, you *are* weak. And when you *feel* strong, you *are* strong. I've done this demonstration hundreds of times, and even I am sometimes surprised at how reliable it is.

Case in point: A few years ago I had the opportunity to do a coaching session with the Baltimore Ravens football team, and one player was kind enough to do this exercise with me. This man is a multiseason NFL player with over a thousand tackles to his credit. He has intercepted and sacked some of the greatest players in the history of the game. He's a walking, talking pillar of physical and mental fitness.

When we began the arm-strength test, I wanted this player to feel strong, and to elicit that feeling, I could have asked him to talk about his physical abilities. But instead I asked him to tap into an even deeper source of positivity: gratitude. I asked him to extend his arm straight out to his side and to not allow me to push it down, no matter what. Then, before attempting to move his arm, I asked him to talk about the people he loves most in the world. He lit up talking about his children and his wife, and when I tried to push his arm down, I got *nowhere*. In fact, if it wasn't for our height difference, I suspect I could have done pull-ups on his arm. The man is all muscle.

But the minute I asked him to say something negative, to bring in doubt, he could not keep his arm up. Truth is, there's not enough muscle in the world to overcome the *idea* that you're weak, or a failure, or unworthy.

This demonstration was a powerful reminder of what I've found to be true time and again: If you think narrative doesn't matter or doesn't shape your reality, it's time to think again. If you tell yourself you're weak, or useless, or not enough, you are going to internalize those thoughts, *right down to your cells*. If you tell yourself you're great, you're strong, you are loved, you're all that and a slice of cake, your cells feel that, too. And they will rally behind you.

Bottom line? Words matter. Your spin on events matters.

The way you've been programmed by the people who love you, hate you, or are indifferent to you? *That only matters when you let it.* The problem is, it's far too easy to let the story somebody else feeds you become the one you live with day in and day out.

———

Over the years, I've jumped at every opportunity to test this concept and see it in action. I use it in my role as an executive coach but also at home with my family and at work with my colleagues. Sometimes it's figurative, but sometimes it's literal. Example: During the ten years I coached my daughters' basketball teams, the girls on my squad all quickly learned that before each game, everybody was going to put their arms up. They knew what I was going to say, but we never, ever skipped it.

Tell me how awesome you are.

Tell me how amazing you are.

Tell me you are strong, powerful women who will absolutely rule the world.

Now you know and I know that it takes more than a pregame ritual to truly empower anyone, but ask yourself: When was the last time you said, out loud, that you are amazing? When was the last time you said you were powerful?

When was the last time you facilitated a situation where someone else could speak their power with absolute confidence that you believed in them?

Those girls, at the age of ten, twelve, fifteen—they built themselves up before every game. I like to think that if they chose to embrace it, the strength they felt during those routines is something they're carrying with them now that they're further down the road—going to college, getting into meaningful relationships, starting careers.

I hope each of them made affirmations of her power part of the story she keeps telling herself.

> *If you tell yourself you're weak, or useless, or not enough, you are going to internalize those thoughts, right down to your cells. If you tell yourself you're great, you're strong, you are loved, you're all that and a slice of cake, your cells feel that, too. And they will rally behind you.*

THE GREAT GAME OF "BANANA"

"Banana" is always the activity of the day in the Sanschagrin family vehicle. Ever since my girls were little, if we were driving, we were playing. I learned this great game from an eight-year-old named Finn. I was visiting a client in Denver, and on the way to a Broncos game, she started playing in the car, explaining the rules as she went. Finn's grown now, but she's still the expert as far as we're concerned—the Banana Commissioner.

When I first picked it up, I saw the game as a simple diversion—a way to pass the time while we made our way from point A to point B—but over the years it's become pretty competitive, and it's taken on more significance for me than just a silly car game. The rules are simple:

> ❯ The game starts when you get in the car and ends when you get where you're going.

> ❭ Along the way, every time you see a yellow car, try to be the first person to point at it and shout *banana!* When you're successful, you earn a point.

> ❭ The banana can be any yellow car, truck, SUV, or even motorcycle, but it can't be a commercial vehicle. No buses, taxis, or delivery vans.

> ❭ Once a vehicle has been called, it can't be called again. So if one of my daughters gets a point for a banana and then I drive around the block and see it again (which I might do if it weren't for this rule—because I'm a serious competitor), I can't re-call it for another point.

> ❭ In the excitement of the game, sometimes mistakes are made. If you shout *banana!* and then realize what you've seen is *not* a banana—for example, if you make a call from far away and then realize it's actually a delivery truck, or that it's orange instead of yellow—then you lose a point.

> ❭ The team with the highest point count on arrival at your destination wins. But if you want to extend the game, you can keep a running count from trip to trip, potentially tallying up scores or even hundreds of bananas.

Technical stuff, right?

Okay. Now how many bananas—i.e., yellow cars—have you seen on the road over the past week?

One? Two? None?

When I ask a live audience, the number is inevitably extremely low.

If you've got this game in your head, how many yellow cars do you think you'll see in the week to come?

I can tell you from experience that it'll likely be a *lot*.

You may wonder how so many yellow cars could possibly exist. And you *may* be inclined to say *banana!* every time you see one. Because the game will be on your mind.

Over the years, I have received no less than a hundred calls, texts, and emails from people who heard me speak and then had follow-up questions about banana. Or who wanted to tell me they were playing. Or who just wanted to say, "Dammit, Chad. Get out of my head," after they'd reflexively pointed at one too many yellow cars.

That's exactly what happened to me after I played that first time in Denver. I kept seeing yellow cars. My logical brain knew they must have been there all along, but I hadn't been noting them.

The game itself is of little consequence. But the fact that with nothing more than an idea, a few rules, and a handful of repetitions of the name, you can train your brain to latch on to something that was always there but never mattered before? That's important.

It's a corollary to what we see in arm-strength testing. In each case, *you find what you focus on.*

HOW IT WORKS: THE BIOLOGY

There are elements of both biology and psychology involved in the "programming" that causes you to notice every yellow vehicle.

The biology is centered in a part of your brain called the reticular activating system, or RAS. This marvel of efficiency constantly, seamlessly sifts through the millions of impressions that come your way all day, every day. In essence, it "screens" each sensory input, each bodily function, and each neurochemical message pinging around your body.

Most of that input is dealt with on automatic. You breathe but don't think about it. You put one foot in front of the other, but you don't have to concentrate. You see what's in front of you but are able to disregard what's in your peripherals, hear what's being said to you but tune out a conversation happening across the room, smell what's on the stove but not that lingering bit of sulfur odor from the broccoli you cooked last night—because your brain knows that's yesterday's news. If you had to deal with every tiny bit of minutia your brain processes with your full attention, you'd be paralyzed by the effort. And so your RAS serves as a sort of gatekeeper, and only when something truly requires your attention does it bring it into your *conscious* awareness. Essentially, you're only getting the headline info—things like: *Something's burning!* or *The baby's crying!* or *I'm hungry!*

The number one function of this system is preserving your safety, so the kinds of inputs that go straight to the front of the needs-attention line generally fall into one of just a few categories: things that are new, things that are sexy, things that are tasty, and *especially* things that are dangerous.

An objective threat like the odor of a toxic chemical, for example, instantly pulls your focus. Or lightning in the sky. Or something that's unexpectedly hot to the touch. This also applies to things that are uniquely alarming to you because of your past experience—like snapping to attention at the sight of every big dog because you once got bit. That's your RAS, sorting business as usual from need to know. This is an amazing tool, with its default settings always on guard for any threat. And whether you think about it or not, it's working all the time.

What's more, it's looped in with the rest of your body—playing a role in how you perceive and react to everything happening around you.

With that in mind, you've got to wonder what might happen if you had the power to tweak the settings. What if you could *decide* what kinds of inputs and impressions come to your attention—or even establish a desirable default reaction? What if you could decide: *I'm going to look for happiness instead of sorrow. I'm going to react with curiosity instead of fear. I'm going to seek the good, the joyful, and the beautiful.*

The fact is, whether you deliberately set about it or not, that's exactly what you do. And that makes you the author of your life.

Think about the last time you had a truly terrible day—not because of any significant tragedy but because you "got off on the wrong foot" or "woke up on the wrong side of the bed." Your alarm didn't sound. The hot water heater was out. Your spouse said something that sounded hurtful.

Off you went thinking: *It's going to be a shitty day.*

And that's exactly what happened.

How does one negative occurrence snowball into a whole cluster of inconveniences, bad experiences, and unhappy feelings? What if, when you determined it was going to be a bad day, your brain responded with: *Okay. Okay, let me find all the ways it's crap.* What if you inadvertently turned on a deep-down goal-seeking mechanism that took your directive and made it happen?

And if you could do that, could you also do the opposite?

This is an idea that's been around for a century, presented in dozens of different ways. From Napoleon Hill's *Think and Grow Rich* in 1937 to Tony Robbins's *Unlimited Power* in 1986 to Rhonda Byrne's *The Secret* in 2006—there's a long shelf of explorations of the ways human beings may be able to control our own fates. Modern science continues to explore the miraculous RAS system but still comes short of fully articulating its precise role in conscious thought. Though we certainly know there is one. Look at hypnosis, the power of suggestion, the laws of attraction—all ways we manipulate and explain away our ability to influence this system.

With even a limited understanding of how it works, though, it's clear that if you can harness the process, then you can use it to help write the life story you want to live.

HOW IT WORKS: THE PSYCHOLOGY

The point at which you make conscious choices to try to drive your RAS is where psychology meets biology. When you start selecting and imprinting words, ideas, and images (which are extremely important, but we'll get to that in a minute), you're essentially picking up your pen and assuming authority over your story.

To do this effectively, you'll start where every narrative ought to start: with theme. What are the themes of your life, and what do you want them to be? It may be the most consequential question most people never think about.

A couple decades ago, if someone had asked me, and if I'd given an honest answer, I would've had to confess that the themes of my life were, in no particular order: *injustice, victimhood, taking care of number one*, and, of course, *having fun*.

I wouldn't have put much effort into choosing. Instead, like my ice cream truck origin story, I'd look at what had settled around me and believe it was my truth. And I didn't mind. Going through life a little ticked off, a little put down, a little selfish, and a lot shortsighted—it all felt comfortable and familiar.

Fast-forward to today, two decades into a long, slow, and ongoing evolution. I have this amazing vocation that allows me the privilege of creating moments that shake listeners up, that open doors to a little clarity and change, and I'm so damned grateful I can hardly stand it. I think about my themes now, about what I'm programming my RAS to deem notable. I *choose* them. And I rededicate myself every day. My list of themes, I realized some time ago, lines up pretty precisely with the list of my values.

It starts with gratitude—the one theme I'd go out on a limb and say that everyone, no matter who you are or what you want, needs to prioritize to help you find happiness.

My own list also encompasses curiosity—because time and time again, the most accomplished and intelligent people I meet are the ones who are *always* willing, even eager, to put themselves in the student's chair.

It includes contribution, because adding value to something bigger than yourself is the quickest path to a sense of fulfillment I know.

My list of themes absolutely hinges on universal respect. Maybe because of my own insecurities, maybe because I worked a lot of service jobs, maybe because the hair on the back of my neck literally stands on end (as in hackles *up*) when I hear someone speak dismissively to a stranger or whisper something ugly about their spouse or kids or colleagues. For whatever reason, this one runs deep for me.

Rounding out the themes that matter most to me—family, faith, and personal growth. I recognize them as nothing less than what I love, what I believe, and what I seek.

Let me tell you, it's a hell of a lot easier to feel fulfilled and successful in this world when I'm operating off that system than it was when I thought everyone and everything was down on me and conspiring to hold me back. Did you know there's an opposite of paranoia? It's called *pronoia*. It's a mindset in which you believe the world is conspiring not to do you harm but to do you good. There's a technical interpretation of this that labels it a delusion—but that's a delusion that could do a lot of good in the world.

The stories you keep telling yourself should all lead you back to the themes and values you hold closest to your heart. When they do, you are constantly bathing your brain in your unique set of principles and priorities—finding and creating congruence on every level.

For example, if my alarm doesn't go off one morning, my story doesn't default to expecting a terrible day ahead. I can find a little gratitude for the extra hour of sleep, make the necessary changes to my commute, my calendar, and my attitude, and move forward with high expectations.

It's a small challenge, dealt with through small adjustments, but there's an essential difference there from the way I would have handled the same problem when I was twenty or thirty or even forty—and it comes down to utilizing every bit of neurobiology I can control in the direction of a good day.

When I can do that, I maintain my authority over my story.

The stories you keep telling yourself should all lead you back to the themes and values you hold closest to your heart. When they do, you are constantly bathing your brain in your unique set of principles and priorities—finding and creating congruence on every level.

THEMES IN PRACTICE

Of course a theme is a big thing to ask your brain to be on the lookout for all the time. If you want to truly utilize your RAS in the most effective ways and keep your central themes at the forefront of your story, you'll need to go beyond theoretical descriptions and figure out what this looks like in real life. You want to be a great parent to your toddler, teen, or adult child? What exactly does that look like and entail? Get specific. Picture it in your mind: What are you doing as a great parent?

You want to excel at sales? What are the images and the sensory experiences that go with that? What does a sales leader do? How does a sales leader come into a meeting, prep a presentation, deliver to a client?

If you want to work on your marriage, start your own company, or break out of a routine that feels stifling to you—what does it look like? How does it sound and feel and smell and taste?

When you commit to this exercise, it is miles beyond daydreaming and simple affirmations. You are giving your brain, your muscles, your emotions, and your cells a directive: *Help me make this happen.*

The proof is in the yellow cars you won't be able to help but see. It's in the muscle-bound arm I can push down with two fingers. There is a tremendous amount of power in deciding what you want to perceive and be.

Now here's the key point: Even when you're not choosing what to seek, this process is ongoing. Your brain is still sifting through an infinite number of sensory inputs. Some you ignore. Some you deal with on an unconscious level. And a small percentage make it past your gatekeeping system and arrive, front and center, in your conscious mind. Knowing that, there are other simple, everyday steps you can take to steer your RAS—even when you're not thinking about it.

One of these is bringing in whatever tools, props, places, or people you believe get you closer to where you want to be. You've heard of dressing for success? Or packing for the trip you want to take? Or walking the walk and talking the talk? All different ways of saying you're preparing your body and mind for the circumstances you want to be true.

This can be as small as what you put in your bag in the morning. When I introduced the concept of the RAS to my daughters, I got them each two notebooks. The first, I told them, was for writing down all the beautiful things they see in the world—examples of kindness and faith and love and humanity. The second was for all the evils—examples of injustice and cruelty and ugliness wherever they saw them.

As I handed them over, I asked the girls, "Which notebook do you think you'll fill first?"

Of course they each had a guess. These are smart girls, plus each has strong opinions about both her own and her sister's personality. A conversation ensued about who is an optimist and who is a pessimist, about what exactly that means, and what's right or wrong about each perspective.

After they hashed it out for a while, I gave them my own opinion—one supported by basically every day of my experience in this world:

"You will fill whichever notebook you pick up on any given day. If you're carrying a notebook for unhappy thoughts, that's what you'll notice. If you're carrying a notebook for beautiful things, you'll fill it up. If you look for how bad the world is, guess what? You're going to find it. If you look for how beautiful it is, then you're going to find that."

Choose which notebook you're going to carry, and you choose which kind of experience you're likely to find.

There are countless small ways you can set up your days to reinforce the themes and stories you want to live.

The secret one I use in my own life? Because I always want to be mindful of the power of the RAS and the programming I can guide, I am *never* in a car where I'm not playing banana. Even when I'm alone.

It's not about winning. It's not about any unusual infatuation with yellow cars. What I love about the game is how it serves as a constant reminder that I get to choose where I put my focus—from what I see and hear to whether I react in anger or amusement, calm or fear. With that in mind, every yellow car I see is a symbol of my power to choose the themes of the days and years of my life. I never want to lose sight of that power, so I keep playing the game.

You find what you focus on.

INCREMENTAL TRUTHS

Of course there are times when it's hard to put your finger on what exactly the execution of your theme should look like. You have a sense of where you want to go—but not a path to get there. This doesn't have to impede your story—it just means you may need to start small. In those moments, you can create momentum bit by bit by committing to small practices that feel like steps in the right direction.

Not sure how to better lead your employees? Start by spending twenty minutes a day reading a management book—soaking in the expertise of people who have walked that path before you. It's twenty minutes. You can do it in bed. You can even listen to the book instead of reading it with your eyes. But if you start today and stick with just this tiny commitment to move toward the theme and value of leadership, in two weeks you'll have soaked up the knowledge one expert has to share. In a month it'll be two. In six months it'll be a dozen, and by then you *will* have a vision of what being a great leader is going to look like for you, and you'll be able to sharpen the target for your RAS.

Another example? You want to heal or deepen a relationship. Maybe you feel your marriage or your relationship with a sibling or one of your children is strained. If you don't know where to start, try saying something kind. I recently watched this unfold with a client—a young, dynamic man who has built a $100 million business empire. He's an amazing, accomplished person. But even with all the great things in his life—professional success, financial security, opportunities to lead—he still suffers.

When we talk about what old photo captures his pain, about what part of his story is a soft spot, he doesn't hesitate. It's his marriage. And the photo is one from a time when he looked at his partner and saw everything he ever wanted. Now he looks at that photo and struggles to remember how that felt. He works late when he doesn't have to. He harbors little resentments that turn into big arguments or long periods of silence.

This is not a new story. The road to great success in business has been paved with broken marriages for at least as long as *tycoon* has been a word, and this man knows that. He deserves props for recognizing the signs of trouble and looking for solutions.

But he had no idea where to begin. Now, I'm not a marriage counselor, but I am a firm believer in both the power of story and the ability to program your RAS, and I had a hunch he could use both to start turning this relationship—which was clearly not past saving—around.

The task I gave him seemed like a simple one: give your wife one unsolicited compliment every day for six months.

One compliment. Easy.

This is a detail-oriented person, and so (not unlike all those people who've followed up regarding the rules of banana) he wanted to know what parameters he should put on it. I told him there weren't any. He didn't need to enlist her help; he didn't need to write them down; he didn't need to do this first thing in the morning or last thing before bed every night.

"You can say, 'I like your shoelaces' if you want," I told him. "But say something, every day."

His response? "That's so dumb, Chad. I can't believe I'm paying you for advice like that."

And I said, "Just do it."

He went away grumbling, but he said he'd follow through.

This "project" didn't get off to a strong start. The first week, my client was shy about it. Which is crazy because he did not get where he is in the world by being shy.

The second week he said he couldn't think of anything nice to say.

The third week he said she was going to know he was "up to something"—which gave me the laugh of the day. We should all be up to something so nefarious.

Finally, as he continued to drag his feet, I said, "The fact that you've been married for decades and you can't do this speaks volumes about your marriage. When we first talked about it, I thought it *might* be a worthwhile exercise for you. But now? I'm certain you need this."

The next week, he did the work of taking a few seconds each day to think of something nice to say and then summoning the nerve to say it.

The first day was okay. So was the second. On the third, he got annoyed because she didn't reciprocate.

I reminded him this was his exercise—not hers. "You're *giving* the compliments, not waiting for them. Just do it."

And so day after day, week after week, month after month, this very busy, very accomplished, and often unhappy man found *something* about his wife to say a few kind words about.

At the six-month mark, he told me things in his marriage had turned around. They were in a really good spot. They were going away for a long weekend, just the two of them without the buffer of the kids and the dogs and constant intrusions from the company. Skiing, at a lodge where the only phone that was going to work was a landline plugged into a wall jack.

I asked if he was still giving daily compliments, and he said, "Yeah, but it's easy now."

Huh.

That's the RAS at work. When this man started this exercise, he'd look at his wife and not *see her*. Instead, he was seeing the tension between them, the arguments, the failure he felt his marriage was becoming. In giving her a compliment every day, he chose to *look for something positive*—and of course there was plenty to choose from. He changed his default from one that was effectively overlooking every good thing in his marriage and about his partner to one seeking and acknowledging positivity. Every day he was successful in doing so, he made an incremental change in the story of their relationship—until the tipping point when he could once again see that yes, of course, the marriage still had magic and could still be the central pillar of his personal life.

Once he got there, it was easy for them to start weaving new stories in their life together.

THE CHOICE

One thing that's been a shocker for me is discovering time and again that most people *don't want* to own this power. It is so much easier to lay your life at the hands of fate and circumstance—to look at every negative that comes your way in terms of what went wrong that was outside your sphere of influence—than it is to write a story that gives you ownership. When you think the source of your troubles is being born in the wrong family, or getting stuck in the wrong career, or being shackled to the wrong partner, then you give up all authority. It's not you. It's not your choices. It's not your story. Most people expect something called *fate* to run the show, and they imagine themselves being pulled along behind it.

Philosopher Carl Jung wrote, "Until you make the unconscious conscious, it will rule your life and you will call it *fate*."

Kind of makes *fate* sound like a dirty word, don't you think? As someone who's been on the other side, who spent a lot of years waiting for the world to tell me who I am and what I'm worth, I choose consciousness all day long.

> *One thing that's been a shocker for me is discovering time and again that most people don't want to own this power. It is so much easier to lay your life at the hands of fate and circumstance, to look at every negative that comes your way in terms of what went wrong, than it is to write the story that gives you ownership.*

QUESTIONS
TO CONSIDER

> What are the themes you want to embody? There's an amazing book by Dr. David Hawkins titled *Power vs. Force*. In it, Hawkins introduces the concept of human beings having a "spectrum of consciousness." At the top? Enlightenment, peace, love. At the bottom? Shame. Guilt. Apathy. Think big as you consider the themes you want to use to shape your narrative. What is most important to you?

> What words, images, or actions can you internalize to engage your RAS in helping you author the best possible

story around those central themes in your life? A photograph? A letter? An object that holds special meaning for you? I have a picture my mother-in-law gave me of her with my daughters, my wife, and my wife's grandmother. Four generations. The minute I looked at that photo, I knew it was something I wanted to make part of my story. *A four-generation picture—with me as the old guy!* I put that on my radar. I could picture it. I wrote it down. I talk about it and think about it. I eat more healthfully, visit the doctor more faithfully, and nurture my relationships more fully because of it. Find ways to keep your most important themes front and center and your mind will find ways to help you stay true to them.

> Where do you need to SHIFT? SHIFT moments are about finding truths, and each of us discovers new ones throughout our lives. As someone who started out in a very dark place and as a coach who often works with people struggling with stagnancy or frustration, I have a lot of opportunity to see these in action (and sometimes to help them along). The big ones?

- The SHIFT from feeling unworthy to knowing you are absolutely worthy of all good things.
- The SHIFT to focusing on the abundance in your life instead of the lack.
- The SHIFT from playing the role of a victim to playing the lead.
- The SHIFT from settling to the bottom to rising to the top.

You don't always have to be at the pinnacle of everything you feel and want and do. But you can always have confidence that your overall trajectory is up. Half the work of making each of these changes is recognizing a need, so check yourself often. When we stop paying attention to how our truth fits with these concepts, we leave room for doubt to seep in.

> How do I command authority over my story? Start by declaring *who you are* and believing it. In doing so, you put your brain and body on a seek-and-find mission for everything that supports that belief. My declaration is I AM a loving and present husband. I AM a devoted and empowering father. I AM a coach who makes a difference. I AM an athlete. I AM a contributor. This is what I am *in the present*, not starting Monday or in January or right after I get back from my trip to Disneyland.

I AM is one of the most powerful phrases in the English language. How do you use it in your declaration?

▪ CANNONBALL BOOK CLUB FAVORITE ▪

The Other Wes Moore: One Name, Two Fates

Wes Moore

CHAD'S NOTE: Since I first fell in love with this book and started recommending it, Wes Moore has gone on to great things, including becoming the governor of Maryland. Long before that happened, though, his book gave me a deeper appreciation for the power of expectation and how it impacts what we focus on. If you expect to fail and everyone around you expects the same, you're dead in the water. But if you expect effort and excellence of yourself—especially if you live in an environment where the people around you expect that, too—then you rise. This true story of two men with the same name, growing up at the same time in similar neighborhoods in the same city, shook my assumptions about how the world works.

It is unsettling to know how little separates us from a different life altogether.

4

SHIFT YOUR ENERGY; FIND YOUR VOICE

We influence with our words. We influence with our actions. But before anything else, we influence with our energy.
When you walk into a room, what emotions come along for the ride?

On a recent trip to the Midwest, I laid out a two-day plan to work with a team I've been coaching for years. It's always amazing to get to spend time with these people and see the great work they're doing. Day one, we had an all-hands seminar—everyone getting together and discussing the state of the company, the success of new initiatives, and what's on the horizon. We shook hands, broke bread, laughed a little, and built community. On the second day, the plan was for the company's president and me to make the rounds to a number of worksites and visit employees on the job.

They'd tell us what was going on in their lives, and we'd help deal with any problems that had come up, reinforce personal connections, answer questions, offer support, and lift morale.

Day one was awesome.

On the morning of day two, I got up before 5 AM, went for a run, grabbed a shower, spoke with my family, and was waiting in the lobby for the president to arrive at 7 AM. When she pulled up, I hustled through the lobby, jumped in the car, and offered a cheerful, booming, "*Morning!* Great to see you again. So looking forward to these visits today. *How are you?*"

In response, I got a little side-eye and a very cool, "Yeah. Morning. How's it going?"

This was, for all intents and purposes, the voice of a different person than the one I'd worked with the day before, the person I have productively collaborated with for years.

So I hopped out of the car and went back in the lobby.

I dialed her number from inside the doors and said, "Good morning! I'm on my way. I'll be out in a sec."

As I folded myself into the passenger seat for a second time, I started fresh. "Hey! How are you? Great to see you."

And she answered, not surprisingly, "What the hell is up with you today?"

What was up was that the energy in that car was all wrong. I said, "Your 'good morning' said it all—said this day is going to be a disaster. I mean, we're on our way to go talk with your people, to be constructive and supportive, to help them feel great about the work they're doing. How are you going to do that? If you want the day to be right, you've got to get your energy right."

Her face fell. "Sorry. It's just been a terrible morning."

So we talked about it. She put a plan in place. And then she moved past it. *Then* we went out and had a kick-ass day in the field.

———

Now, we could talk about unreasonable expectations to be cheerful, or how the idea of reading a person's energy is too woo-woo for some people, or even about how *maybe* my enthusiasm can be a bit forward in the morning. But here's the bottom-line truth:

Energy is our greatest resource, and because of that, it's something I don't fool around with. In that moment, I knew we were either going to have a do-over or a wasted day in the field. I chose the former.

A lot of people talk about energy as if it's something that just happens to us. But that's not true. The energy you bring to any given moment is something you can 100 percent control. You can own it, and you can change it.

I know it well, because at the end of the day, one of the biggest things I bring to the table as both a speaker and as a coach is my energy. People don't collaborate with me because of my academic pedigree or my quirky genius. What they connect with me for and remember me by is my energy. To be honest, one of the great fears I had in sitting down to work on a book was that the energy I bring to a room might not translate to the page. If you can't feel my energy, if you can't feel what I'm feeling when I tell you a story or ask about your life, then we're not connected.

And man, do I treasure that connection.

When I share something about my life and you share something back, and we can each take away a little bit of the other's experience: that's pretty close to magic.

It's my job as a speaker to bring that magic—and sometimes my job as a coach is to help you get your own energy right.

> *A lot of people talk about energy as if it's something that just happens to us. But that's not true. The energy you bring to any given moment is something you can 100 percent control. You can own it, and you can change it.*

TWO RULES

Energy is our fuel, and it's also something we equate with our essence. When you meet someone who has obvious great energy, sometimes you know you like them right away. And sometimes you encounter people with so much negative energy you can feel it rolling off them.

What could be more important than that?

Your energy tells your story in countless subtle ways—through your facial expressions, your gestures, your eye contact, where you put your attention, and especially in your voice. Your words, tone, volume—even your silences convey your unique and personal vibe.

It's amazing how careless people get with that. The voice you use to keep telling yourself what you're capable of or how you feel or what went wrong or what went right with your day—it can be the defining factor in how you internalize that experience (let alone how everyone around you hears it).

My family has two house rules when it comes to this subject:

Rule Number One is that you have a moral obligation to leave any room with better energy than it had when you came in. It's the ultimate take on the old adage: *If you don't have anything nice to say, don't say anything at all.*

This is not always easy. Everybody has bad days, and some days what you think you most need is to dump all your garbage into somebody else's lap. We've all done it—spewing anger or bitterness or misery *just to get it out.* We've also been the vampire—drawing away whatever positive energy exists in a room with negative comments or a refusal to give our attention or affection.

But what happens if you take a pause before you launch into either overwhelming an exchange with your crap or creating a vacuum with your lack of focus? What if you take one moment before you cross the threshold to think: *Hang on a sec. Is this really what I want to bring to these people I care about and respect?*

What else have I got?

I don't just practice this at home. I practice it everywhere. It doesn't mean I'm a Pollyanna. Just like everyone else, I have a dark side I regularly have to contend with. It doesn't mean I don't ever get angry or gloomy and need to talk things through. It means I know it's within my power to shift my energy—to do whatever work is necessary to get centered and positive and grateful. (I'll walk you through some of the ways that work gets done in a minute.)

Rule Number Two is a simple declarative statement—one that pulled me straight out of that car at 7 AM when there was obviously trouble brewing: *I can't be with you if I'm leaving with less energy than I had coming into this exchange.*

You may not know or care that you're draining me, but I know. I care.

Here's how it plays out on a bad day: As I was writing this chapter, I had a scheduled call with a coaching client who is the ultimate man's man. He works in construction. He's built a business empire. He skis, climbs mountains, hunts wild boar. He fears nothing.

He's kind of a force of nature.

Except that on this day, as on a few others before it, that force was hostile. He was pissed off—angry at so many people and practices and rules and circumstances that I didn't bother trying to keep up. He was on a tear, and his energy was gruff, miserable, borderline menacing. In the moment, not only was he building a massive, jagged wall between himself and everyone around him, but he was heaving sticks and stones over that wall while he did it.

There are times when a coach's role is to sit back and ask questions, to wait for thoughtful answers, to gently guide a process of discovery and transformation.

This was not one of those times. The interruption of this energy spiral needed to be blunt, and it needed to be quick.

I told him the truth. "You are failing, miserably, in every area of your life that's important to you right now. How many people have you done this to today? This week? You're pushing everyone away. You're insulting your employees. You're being disrespectful to your family. You're acting paranoid. And you've somehow got the idea that the people who care about you and are trying to help—people who have always looked out for you in the past—no longer have your back."

Of course, because this was a hell of a mood, that turned his attention to me, starting in with a line of complaints centered around: "You don't know what I have to deal with . . ."

If I had a nickel for every time I'd heard someone say those words or some corollary of them ("This always happens to me," "You wouldn't believe how hard it is," and even the classic and childish, "This is so unfair")—well, I'd have at least a few dollars. Doubling down on not being responsible for how you feel should not be that common.

EVOLUTION OF AN EMOTION

So let's break this down—this wild roller-coaster ride that takes someone from a seconds-long incident that pisses them off all the way to the ragged edge of an unpleasant personality. You've seen it in action, right? If you have the questionable fortune of working or living with someone who has a nasty temper, you may see it all the time.

Let's talk about how it happens.

Rage, that moment when something occurs and you absolutely see red—that's biological. One of the oldest, most automatic parts of your brain perceives danger or a threat and fires up *immediately*. This is an asset, because it allows you to fight or run or defend your child or swerve around a car accident.

But how long it lasts once that immediate threat is gone? How and when you deal with it? Those things are up to you.

The natural lifespan of that rage response is a few seconds to a few minutes—unless you feed it. When we take that jolt of fear or anger, nurse it for twenty minutes, keep telling ourselves how furious we are—then we get into something bigger, something worse: a *mood*. By then we've also got that shitty day we talked about in chapter 3—and we've got our RAS programmed to find all possible evidence that it's going to stay that way.

Next up? Well, the worst course of action is carrying that mood around all day, maybe coming home and unloading it on the family, then taking it to bed—thereby risking "waking up on the wrong side of the bed" in the morning. Another shitty day . . .

The biggest problem with this, the biggest danger, is that if we aren't careful about how we let our emotions and moods rule our lives, if we let fear or anger or desolation program our RAS and by default write our stories, then one day they may become our *personality*.

I'm willing to bet that if you and I were sitting together having this conversation, you'd be able to tell me about someone in your life who has gone through this terrible transformation. Someone who has let negative forces control them to the point where they have actually *become* a negative force. Someone with utterly lousy energy.

You can't let that happen. You have another moral obligation here—to guard against letting your energy go dark.

Here's a secret it took me decades to learn—perhaps the one I most wish I'd figured out sooner: *You have it within you to stop feeding any emotion and let it go.* That doesn't mean you have to be happy all the time. We all need to experience our grief, our frustration, and our longing. We need the full gamut of emotions to keep us on a path of learning and growth. But if an emotion is not serving you in some way, you can choose not to feed it. Anger about somebody cutting me off in traffic? Why would I want to waste any of my precious energy on that? Bitterness toward someone who beat me to a promotion or rejected my application or turned down my proposal? It's going to come for me, and I am going to turn it away.

I no longer feed emotions I don't want to sustain. That one SHIFT has changed my life, brought me peace, and helped me cultivate a big, powerful, positive energy that propels my endeavors and my relationships: an energy that's catching.

ENERGY AND VOICE

When we talk about voice in a narrative, we're talking about the energy that comes with the words and the story. It's the tone, the attitude, the resonance, the playfulness or anger or concern or authority. It's all the emotion and history that informs what you're saying and doing. There is no combination of words you can't change completely based on the energy with which you deliver them. And every time you put something out in the world, you are either deliberately choosing that voice or you're unconsciously choosing it.

Ditto for your nonverbal expression. Say the same thing with an eye roll that you do with a handshake or a hug and you get a completely different meaning.

One of the hot topics that frequently comes up with my coaching clients—including the irate fellow I introduced a couple pages back—is that they forget (or deliberately disregard) the fact that their voice and their energy are constantly impacting the people around them. You can use these tools to put people at ease or to put them on edge. You can empower or belittle. You can draw someone closer or push them away.

So please, be deliberate. Know your power. Pay attention to how people are responding to you. Your voice and your energy are among the greatest tools you have in your power to cultivate relationships and make things happen.

> *One of the hot topics that frequently comes up with my coaching clients is that they forget (or deliberately disregard) the fact that their voice and their energy are constantly impacting the people around them. You can put people at ease or put them on edge. You can empower or belittle. You can draw someone closer or push them away.*
>
> *So please, be deliberate. Know your power.*

QUESTIONS
TO CONSIDER

> ❯ What kind of energy do you bring to a room? Do you make it better? If not, how can you SHIFT it so you're a positive force? Sometimes all it takes is a quiet moment—a chance to get your head together, take a deep breath, and focus on what's ahead of you instead of what's behind. Sometimes you need more: a constructive conversation or a hike, run, or yoga class. Or putting on a soundtrack that evokes good times. Or just getting outdoors. Find the tools that help you pivot from focusing on everything that's going wrong to all that's right with the world. What's your go-to pivot point?

> ❯ Is your voice drawing people toward you—because you're strong, funny, smart, charming, empowering, a great teacher or leader? Or is it possible that your voice is push-ing people away—because it's angry or bitter or jealous or bored or superior or bossy? No one's voice is the same all the time, but most of us have patterns. Pay attention to

how people respond to you. Ask people you trust for feed-back. Cultivate the voice and energy you want to project instead of letting them happen *to* you.

> What kinds of voices do you love to hear and learn from? What kind of energy do you love to be around? Is there someone in your life you can study as your own voice and energy continue to evolve (which, if you're doing it right, should be ongoing for the rest of your life)? A few years ago when I started my podcast, I had a long list of reasons I wanted to have that in my life. I wanted to get access to interesting people. I wanted to explore topics that fascinate me. I wanted to think more deeply. I wanted to be heard.

  - One thing that wasn't on my list but has become one of the most tremendous benefits of the experience is how it's allowed me to study voice and energy. Every time I sit down with one of these amazing, accomplished people, I take a minute to let the thrill of the event hit me, and then I start studying the energy that comes with the person. How do they carry themselves? How do they look at me? How do they pause? When do they push ahead with a statement and when do they stop for a question? What words and gestures do they keep coming back to? The more opportunities I have to do this, the more I'm aware of my own energy, my own voice, and my potential to make an impact.

> Who do you know who demonstrates great energy? What are they teaching you?

• CANNONBALL BOOK CLUB FAVORITES •

The Four Agreements: A Practical Guide to Personal Freedom
Don Miguel Ruiz

CHAD'S NOTE: *The Four Agreements* lives on my personal Mount Rushmore of books. I'm aware this book is one of the bestsellers of recent history, but I couldn't bring myself to leave it out of this discussion. It is deceptively easy to read and digest—but, man, are its principles difficult to put into practice. I defy any reader to come away from this book without recognizing areas in their life where they need work and then finding new resolve to do that work. This title is applicable to every person at every stage of life. I believe it's one of the best leadership books, best relationship books, best self-help books, and best parenting books ever written.

> *Go inside and listen to your body, because your body will never lie to you.*
> *Your mind will play tricks, but the way you feel in your heart, in your guts, is the truth.*

When Things Fall Apart

Pema Chödrön

CHAD'S NOTE: One more from my Mount Rushmore of books—and a book that's well on its way to being read by everyone in the world. Chödrön is a monk who writes eloquently about the idea that when things are at their worst, when we most need to overcome, we have the ability to change our thoughts anytime we want. We can stop the bleeding. This was a big-think book for me, and it's one I frequently share. No instance of that stands out more than when I gave a copy of this title to a guest who was kind enough to come on my podcast. I'd chosen it with care, thinking, *She'll love this like I do.* But I was not prepared for the moment when she pulled this book out of her gift bag and hugged it, her eyes brimming with tears.

She said, "This book saved my life."

So yes, I'm sure she already had a copy, but the universe seemed to bless the moment all the same.

Letting there be room for not knowing is the most important thing of all.

When there's a big disappointment, we don't know if that's the end of the story.

It may just be the beginning of a great adventure.

5

SET THE STAKES

Great stories have high stakes.
What is your impact? Why does it matter?

As a speaker, I often share my best- and worst-case scenarios for any given talk during my first few minutes with an audience. The dream? True connection. Somebody who laughs and cries, feels moved to action, and follows through. If I get that, even from one person, I go home happy.

Second best? A moment of grief and self-assessment. Or a big laugh at something you know hits home. Or a vow to make a change—even one you're going to forget in a couple days.

The next rung down on this scale is *any* emotion. Sad? Fine. Frustrated? Okay. Angry you spent forty-five minutes in my company that you'll never be able to get back? I won't love that, but I'll take it all day long over the lowest rung: indifference.

Because a story that you're indifferent to is not a story at all. It's just mumbling, or static, or white noise. If all you hear from me is *blah, blah, leadership,* then I've let you down. And we both might just as well have stayed in bed.

A narrative's stakes are perhaps the most critical and necessary element. They're the part of a story, or a speech, or even an action that defines *what's on the line.* They're why you care. Sometimes the stakes of the stories you keep telling yourself are blatantly obvious—you're keeping someone safe; you're helping the company stay afloat; you're earning a paycheck; you're bringing that blood pressure down; you're setting an example for your kids.

Sometimes, though, stakes are more subtle—like whether you feel a sense of self-worth at the end of the day; or whether you're moving a little closer to making a connection with another person or moving further away; or whether you're putting your whole heart into the task at hand or barely showing up. When the stakes are low, it's easy to struggle with your *why*—to wonder *what's the point?*

One thing I know for sure, whether you're pushed by your fears or your hopes or your cravings or your aversions: without sufficient stakes in any given story, sooner or later you're going to reach indifference.

As a coach, I meet people all the time who've never given much thought to the stakes of their stories—and others who've looked for them and come up empty. Some will go so far as to openly state that the work they do isn't relevant. Or that the efforts they're making as a parent probably aren't getting through. Or that, truth be told, they're mostly just going through the motions with their spouse.

It's easy to say those things and sound nonchalant, but deep down, we all know they hurt. It's part of the human experience to want our actions and our existence to *matter.*

And so I often find myself, in an early coaching session, asking what I believe to be a critical question: *Does what you do matter?*

We have that conversation because we can't talk about changing the things you keep telling yourself without acknowledging that the stakes of your stories are absolutely consequential. Epic, even.

Too much? I don't think so. Just as small stories can loom large, seemingly low stakes can become dire over time. If you don't feel invested in the effort you're making, the work you're doing, and the stories you're telling, you're always going to have a fulfillment gap. It's yet another form of the suffering that comes from knowing you're capable of more but settling for less. And it can be contagious. Don't give a damn about the work you do or the event your family's having or whether you take care of yourself? Then the people who work with you, live with you, and spend time with you will read that indifference. If you're in a leadership role, they may internalize it, thinking: *If they don't care, then why should I?*

Not surprisingly, losing sight of the stakes of the shared story is one of the fastest and most effective ways to run a corporate culture right into the ground.

So when you think about the heft of your story, know that its stakes are nothing less than your happiness and fulfillment—and that you're either contributing to or taking away from the stakes the people around you put into their stories, too.

See? Epic. Those stakes are sky-high.

It's so easy to think your story doesn't matter when you live in a world populated by billions, when you follow a predictable routine, when your everyday contributions seem to go unnoticed. But let's take one minute for a reality check. Who are the people who've had the most profound impacts on your life?

Maybe you've got Billy Joel or Michael Jordan or Eleanor Roosevelt on your list, but chances are most of the people who've profoundly influenced you aren't household names. They're people just doing their jobs, following their routines, and showing up. A parent or grandparent, mentor or teacher, coach or faith leader— maybe even the carrier who whistles down your street every day delivering mail or the old aunt who never forgets your birthday.

These people are not all giants in this world. They're men and women who get out of bed in the morning and do whatever they do with some level of trust that it matters.

> *If you don't feel invested in the effort you're making, the work you're doing, and the stories you're telling, you're always going to have a fulfillment gap.*

"JUST A JOB"

The place where this gets sticky is usually at the office. For a lot of people, the stakes of their professional stories are hard to pin down.

A while back I spent the day coaching a group of sales executives at an apparel company in my hometown of Baltimore. They make kids' sports uniforms.

We had a good day, productive and genial and full of upbeat energy. But late in the afternoon, I asked one of the senior salesmen a question, and things got quiet.

"Matt, do you believe what you do matters?"

He asked for clarification. "What do you mean, *matters*?"

"I mean, in the grand scheme of life, do you believe that what you do *matters*? Is it important?"

Matt looked at me for a second, considering, I'm sure, how to answer honestly without sounding dismissive. And he may have been wondering why I'd poke at this potentially sensitive spot.

"Listen, Chad," he said, his face somber. "I love your training. It's been awesome. I've learned a lot. But if you're asking me if what I do is changing the world? Then no. I don't have a huge impact. I sell uniforms."

I asked how that made him feel, and he told me it was *fine*, that his job enables him to put food on the table for his family—his highest priority. But, he clarified, he doesn't go out in the world every day curing diseases or putting out fires. His impact, he said, doesn't move the needle on the scale of contribution.

His answer summed up, I suspect, how most people feel about their work. *I'm a good person making a good living for a good reason.* It's a decent story, a decent life. Maybe it can get to feeling a little hollow or stale, but we want it to be enough.

But I believe that every job, every career, every company is a platform to do something meaningful—that if you look for high stakes, you will find them. When you roll them into your story, you'll find you can do more with that platform than you ever thought possible.

Now Baltimore, a city I love, has been through some extremely tough times. It's had more than its share of crime and poverty and unrest. Matt knew that as well as I did as we continued our conversation—him ready for me to move on to the next topic and me hoping I could help him SHIFT his perspective.

"I appreciate you sharing your experience," I told him. "Can we take a minute to look at this from another angle?"

He nodded. "Sure."

"Right now," I said, "somewhere in this city there's a ten-year-old getting home from school. This is a kid who lives in an area where it's not safe for him to walk on the street after sundown. He doesn't always know where his next meal is coming from. He goes to a school that doesn't have the resources to provide him with the quality of education he deserves.

"He's being raised by a single parent who works two jobs. He knows he's loved, but he spends a lot of time alone. At night, sometimes he sleeps on the floor, because he hears gunshots out in the neighborhood and that terrifies him.

"Do you think there's a boy in the city in that situation right now?" I asked.

"Without question," Matt said solemnly.

"Agreed," I continued. "Now every Saturday, this kid gets to wear a football uniform, and run out on the gridiron, and hear people cheer his name. In those moments, he feels *important* and *special* and *strong*. That uniform is the closest thing he has to a Superman cape. And every chance he gets, he wears it to school, too, because that's where and how he feels most significant in his world right now.

"Your company made that Superman cape. You got it into that child's hands. And for a couple days a week, when he wears it and feels important, you are part of his story and he is part of yours."

We sat quiet for a beat, thinking about this imaginary child who represents a lot of very real boys and girls in our communities. And then I asked Matt, "If that's the story you tell yourself, *then* do you think that what you do matters?"

Now Matt is a big guy, in his fifties. His face crumpled, and he wiped his eyes. And he said he'd never thought about it that way. But now that he was, yeah, maybe the work he was doing was of greater consequence than he was giving himself credit for.

This exchange, for the record, is part of the stakes of *my* story as a coach and a speaker, too. A grown man cried, challenged his own assumptions, changed the story he'd been telling himself for more than a decade, and raised the stakes of how he spends his days. SHIFT moments like that are the reason I dive into the work I am privileged to do every day.

The next time I saw Matt, he'd made a slew of changes. He'd become his company's top performer. He'd built new relationships with sports organizations in the city. He carried himself like a guy who was going places.

And he did. In fact, he founded his own company—one centered on the premise that childhood sports give kids a chance to feel like superheroes.

This was a great man who immediately took ownership of a story that gave him more power to do good in his community and ran with it.

———

I believe that every person in this world has a unique platform from which to contribute—a place from which they can do great work. But I meet people all the time who think their efforts, their work—even their relationships—have no stakes. I've lost track of how many times I've felt compelled to ask: *What makes you think that your job doesn't matter?*

Or the question that may cut deepest: *Do you really believe the words you say don't have impact? That your actions aren't making an impression on someone in your orbit?*

Sometimes it just takes asking the question to wake you up to the stakes of your stories. But sometimes you have to dig deeper to find the catalyst that allows you to appreciate the scope of your impact—which directly correlates to your sense of self-worth.

When you understand and believe in the impact you can have, it changes you. When you find that magical place where your purpose and your unique path for fulfilling it come together, you don't need me or anybody else to rain tools over you. You'll go find whatever systems, processes, and tools you need.

STAKES TOO HIGH? WHEN OVERESTIMATION IS HOLDING YOU BACK

Let's flip this script. Because just as there are times when we underestimate the stakes of our actions, there are times when we overestimate them as well. I frequently meet with coaching clients who've convinced themselves they can't do something that's important to them because it's too much, too big a commitment. And sometimes the SHIFT that needs to happen is realizing that giving something a shot, taking a chance, dedicating some small amount of your energy is *not* going to derail the rest of your life.

Case in point: I have a coaching client who lives in the South-west and runs a company he built from scratch. It's growing every day. He's young and brilliant; he's hardworking; he has a beautiful, loving family.

What he doesn't have, or so he keeps telling himself, is time to take care of his health. He told me so, week after week and month after month. Now, as a coach, it's not my job to tell you what is important to you or worth your time. It's my job to help you see those things for yourself—to trip over the truth. In this case, it didn't take Sherlock Holmes to see what this guy was suffering over—and he wasn't so much failing to trip over his truth as walking into it over and over again like so much brick wall.

When I asked what the problem was, he gave me the usual. *I'm too busy. My company needs me. My family needs me.*

All true. And yet . . . when you tune in to the stories you keep telling yourself and continually find the same point of complaint—of suffering—it's time to take action. When we attended a professional conference together, I decided it was time to help the process along.

And that's why I have in my possession a photo of this man lying on a sandy beach in Florida glaring up at me. He's not sipping a margarita or topping off his tan or taking in a spectacular sunset. No. He's clutching his guts, guzzling water, and cursing a blue streak—because we went running together, and the physical exertion kicked his ass.

He'd convinced himself it was impossible for him to make time to take care of his health. And so when we were on the trip, I suggested he come for just one run. One time. One day. He demurred—so busy, so tired. But it was the "one" that got him. I mean, here we both were, on the same schedule in the same city.

Now, it does not matter to me one bit if this man takes up running or not. What matters to me is that a big chunk of the frustration in his life was tied to his poor health—with knowing that already, in his thirties and at the top of his professional game, he was feeling physically depleted.

The headline of that day was that he got out of bed, went for a run, and was still able to honor all his commitments. In fact, he was on fire.

Two days later, he got out of bed and ran again. And two days after that.

Back at home, he discovered that if he was careful and quiet getting out of the house, he could run there, too. Today he covers three miles, three times a week. As a habit. Nothing is lost from his schedule. Nothing is lost from his marriage or his relationship with his kids. He's no more tired than he was when he was getting that extra hour of sleep. In fact, now his energy is up. He doesn't get winded climbing a flight of stairs. The chronic back pain he'd been dealing with is gone.

The high stakes of making the small commitment to do something about it, it turns out, were mostly in his head.

The rule of thumb here is this: High stakes in your story should pull you in and propel you forward. But if the perception of high stakes is keeping you locked up, go ahead and take a chance. Push a limit. See what you can do.

QUESTIONS
TO CONSIDER

> What are the stakes of the stories you keep telling yourself? Are they high enough?

> How do your professional interactions and contributions matter? Look at them from every angle. What resonates with you? Your impact on a company? On an industry? On people who look to you for leadership?

> What about your personal relationships? How are you impacting the people you love most with your assumptions, your words, and your actions?

> Are you raising the stakes in the right places (and choosing not to sweat the small stuff in others)? Where can you shuffle emphasis to bring your priorities more in line with the story you want to tell?

> How can you facilitate another person coming to appreciate that the work they do or the energy they put into the world matters? Doing this for someone else will not only be an act of kindness, it'll help keep the themes and values of your own life front and center.

▪ CANNONBALL BOOK CLUB FAVORITE ▪

**The Gap and the Gain: The High Achievers' Guide
to Happiness, Confidence, and Success**

Dan Sullivan with Dr. Benjamin Hardy

CHAD'S NOTE: You know you've stumbled on a great and timely book when you think as you're reading that it could have been written just for you. That was this title for me. I lived in what Sullivan and Hardy call "the gap" for a long time—always focused on what I had not accomplished instead of on what I'd done well. I have a tendency to slip back into that mindset even now. This book created a SHIFT for me, helping me learn to utilize positive measurements instead of negative ones. It's been invaluable in helping me set the stakes for my own efforts and stories.

> *The way to measure your progress is backward against where you started, not against your ideal.*

6

FREE YOUR MASTERPIECE

Measure what you've gained but also all you shed along the way.

Is your life's plot about embracing possibilities or burying flaws?

I meet a lot of people who plot their days, and sometimes much of their lives, around compensating for their shortcomings and imperfections. Some lack self-esteem, so they deflect attention at any cost. Others (also, ironically, lacking self-esteem) over-compensate by cultivating giant egos. Some aggressively manage employees to keep scrutiny from themselves. Some shy away from leadership, worried it will expose what they don't know or can't do. And many—most, even—choose to keep their lives and aspirations in narrow lanes, because they're so sure they couldn't be successful anywhere else.

Most of us know how this feels. We've been there—maybe for a few days, maybe every day. We've been so caught up in hiding our weaknesses that we forget we even have strengths. Or we forget to be kind. Or we forget that sometimes staying in a rut is worse than trying (and even failing) at something exciting and challenging.

It's part of a coach's job to pull at these threads—to wonder if and why you and I and my clients are limiting ourselves. I often open that dialogue by sharing one of the greatest SHIFT moments of my own life—one that played out in front of a hundred strangers in a crowded Italian museum.

It was the year I turned forty, and I'd won a big sales award from the homebuilder I was working for—one that came with a substantial travel voucher. I could book through the corporate travel agency to go anywhere I wanted.

Anywhere in the world.

Things like this did not happen in my life. When I looked inward, even though by that time I was a high-achieving sales exec, I still saw a guy who was barely getting by. In all honesty, the first time I received a big commission in a paycheck, I called the company's accounting office to report an error.

"I'm sorry, Chad," the manager told me. And I thought: *Of course. I'll have to give this back.* But as she kept talking, it seemed she was apologizing because the number was low, because part of that commission would be coming in my next check. There'd been some kind of paperwork error and the net outcome would be *in my favor.*

Even after I hung up, the whole scenario didn't quite compute.

Ditto for this amazing reward from the company. I wasn't sure it was legit. I wanted to use that voucher right away in case somebody wised up to their mistake. After some debate with my wife about whether we'd dare go off on a big trip and leave our two young daughters at home, I took a deep breath and booked us a twelve-day European cruise. It would be, I was sure, the adventure of a lifetime.

When the time came for us to embark, I was as excited as I'd ever been in my life. I'd seen photos of the places we were about to visit—the Leaning Tower of Pisa, the blue domes of Santorini, the basilicas of Florence, the Vatican—but I could barely wrap my head around being on my way to experience them in person. I'd never dreamed travel like that could be in my cards.

At every port, I'd hustle off the ship, gather our transfer and attraction tickets, and situate myself for perfect views. I'd grin ear to ear and get a little misty with gratitude. You should only be allowed to use the word *wow* so many times in a single trip, but I nearly wore it out.

Florence was one of the last stops, and for me (and most of my fellow travelers), it was all about seeing the city's world-famous artworks. I hired a driver to take us to a museum, and as we walked among the painted Madonnas and angels, crucifixion scenes and biblical figures, I felt I was seeing stories from my Catholic upbringing in a new, vivid light.

But I knew—everyone in the place knew—that the exhibit we'd set out to see was Michelangelo's *David*, so we kept pushing forward.

The final approach to the *David* is lined with a series of Michelangelo's unfinished works—statues of men historians have dubbed "the prisoners." Because they're incomplete, these sculptures seem to depict their subjects actively emerging from stone, eternally half-formed and half-freed. It's an eerie, awesome sight, and it makes it all the more stunning when you reach the vaulted end of the gallery and find yourself, finally, staring up at the *David*—who is as fully realized as a figure who is not flesh and blood can possibly be.

Now, I'd seen this statue in pictures before our trip. I'd seen it on postcards in the shops we'd passed that morning. I'd had a vague notion of what to expect, but the image in my head was predicated on my experience of a few small-scale photographs and on my familiarity with the David and Goliath story. With those in mind, I'd expected to see a statue that represented some sort of handsome everyman. I mean, when we talk about David and Goliath, David's not the imposing one. He's not the one who made hardened soldiers cower. That's all Goliath—it's giant stuff. David was the underdog, a shepherd, the little brother of his family. He was armed with a *slingshot,* for heaven's sake.

But *the David* (and standing at its feet I suddenly understood why we continue to refer to Michelangelo's version that way) is no everyman. He's magnificent. At seventeen feet tall, he *is* a giant— one so artfully carved from a single block of marble that he appears to be on the verge of motion. Unlike the prisoner statues, there's not an ounce of excess stone on his form. You can almost see him breathing, see veins and muscles shift beneath his skin. Tourists come into that space thinking they're just going to see the statue and walk on by; but most, like me, stay put, transfixed—trying to comprehend how this five-hundred-year-old work of art has overwhelmed our senses.

When a tour group stopped beside me and the guide began to speak, I leaned in, eavesdropping in hopes of learning more about the statue.

The docent, speaking in heavily accented English, explained that the massive block of marble was first commissioned to two other artists. Both of them struggled with it—so much so that at one point, the stone was deemed too flawed to become a worthwhile work of art. With the sculpting barely begun, the project was abandoned for decades.

Michelangelo was just twenty-six years old when he took it up. He labored over that "flawed" stone for the better part of three years, working largely in seclusion at his workshop. When the statue was nearly finished, it was so big it took four days and forty workers to move it the half mile to its original home in a city plaza.

The docent said that when the statue reached the plaza and was set upright, a small child pulled at Michelangelo's hem and asked how he'd made something so perfect and beautiful from a plain stone.

This story was presented as fact but was probably legend. And that guide probably shared it with fifty tourists or more every single day—tourists who kept their composure just fine. But when she lowered her voice, as if to echo the sculptor's answer to the child, and said, "*It was there all along. I only carved away the edges to reveal it,*" a slow-rolling flood of emotions washed over me with so much force I nearly dropped to my knees.

My face crumpled and my shoulders hunched. I started weeping in sloppy, noisy sobs—prompting my wife to look up in alarm and the tour group to start moving away. A few of them glanced back at me with concern as they went.

It was there all along.

It was there all along.

I replayed the words, imagining them coming from the artist, imagining him believing that he was as much excavating his art as creating it. I imagined perfect forms encased in marble, waiting to be freed.

It took a few minutes to compose myself and put words to what I was feeling. The truth is, standing there beneath a statue that's been a standard of artistic perfection for centuries, hearing that the sculptor believed the masterpiece always existed within the stone—I caught the whisper of a metaphor for my life.

For decades, the main plotlines of my story centered on the ways I was trying to ignore, bury, and overcome what I understood to be my innate flaws and shortcomings. I'd covered unhappiness by being a smart-ass. I'd covered insecurity about my intelligence by getting as far as I could from the world of academia. I'd covered my tendency to play the victim by embracing shallow relationships where no one would ever call me on it. Even at forty, with so much going my way, I still expended ridiculous amounts of my energy covering, covering, covering.

In chapter 2, I used the analogy of our stories building up like so many layers of rock or stone around us, settling, sealing us in. This was the moment I began to see my life that way. I had built up *so much* rock. No father? Rock. No education? Rock. No money? Rock. Every terrible, sad story I'd ever told that set me up for failure was another layer. Over time, I'd accumulated what felt like tons of "cover-up" narrative—all of it based on the core premise that I was unworthy of a happy and fulfilling life. That if anyone ever got a look at the "real" me, they'd be repelled.

The SHIFT that day, the most unexpected stumble over truth of my life, was buried in the statues—in those half-encased prisoners along the hall, and in the towering, gleaming *David*. I'd always believed I was born broken, and I'd made a long, slow transition from a kid who felt utterly worthless to a man constantly pinching myself to make sure the good life I was living was actually mine. I worried, constantly, that the universe would correct its error and call everything back.

But in that moment I considered—perhaps for the first time—whether maybe the plot of my life didn't have to be built around hiding my failings. Maybe it could be about freeing, embracing, and honing some best version of myself. Maybe instead of being born broken, I'd come into the world perfect and pure.

The first wave that hit me was one of regret. I'd been fighting a deep-seated sense of self-loathing for nearly forty years. And for what? For nothing? Had I spent decades trying to bury parts of me—my personality, my thought process, my instincts—that might be worthy of acknowledgment?

The second wave was one of possibility, because every cell in my body was keyed up—because the way all this was adding up felt true. I was figuring it out at the feet of the *David*, but the pieces that were falling into place had always been on the periphery of my life, waiting to be put together. It felt true enough that I was ready to start asking questions, to start chiseling, to start reevaluating my worth.

The last wave of emotion to hit was one of relief. I felt as if I'd come to a big reveal in the story of my life, and even in the moment I recognized how damned lucky I was to have it happen when I was forty, instead of fifty, or eighty. Or never.

Now I had to figure out what to do with it. I knew the answers would be more complicated than the revelation. I knew I was going to have to let go of my obsession with being damaged goods—a task that's easy to speak but hard to do.

It's no exaggeration to say deciding I was good enough *right down to my core* that day changed every plotline of my life. As I wiped my face, kissed my wife, stood to my full height, and took one last long look at the *David*, I felt lighter, smarter, and more hopeful than I could ever remember feeling before. It was the beginning of a new chapter.

> *I'd made a long, slow transition from a kid who felt utterly worthless to a man constantly pinching myself to make sure the good life I was living was actually mine . . . In that moment at the David, I wondered if maybe the plot of my life didn't have to be built around hiding my failings. Maybe it could be about freeing, embracing, and honing some best version of myself.*

CHISELING TO POSSIBILITY

As we go through our lives, we all have this kind of "rock" grow up around us, binding us. It happens in such subtle, silent ways, right from childhood, that it's no wonder that sometimes it takes a mind-bending moment to recognize it. It's so easy to allow your perceived shortcomings to define the way you see yourself. I'd be willing to bet that as you read this you can think of a formative moment when you *know* this happened to you. A few examples:

> ❯ A friend whose fourth-grade teacher wrote in her report card, "J's let-my-talent-carry-me attitude is unbecoming." The child was *nine* when she brought that note home—a straight-A-plus student who hadn't yet gotten comfortable with the fact that academics came easily to her. Forty years later she still gets the same kicked-in-the-teeth feeling

when she thinks of that note and the way it made her stop raising her hand.

- As a father who's spent the better part of twenty years trying to foster SPW (strong powerful woman) energy in my daughters, I'm blown away by this particular layer of rock and the idea of telling a little girl not to act too smart.

> A client who's a born leader—one with work crews that would follow him to the ends of the earth (and that always do amazing work)—was told by an early boss that success is "measured in degrees." Since my client has no higher education, the employer then overtly stated there would be no upward mobility in his career. As someone who's walked this path—learning over decades that leadership and formal education do not always go hand in hand—it was easy for me to recognize how this layer of rock had kept this man committed to living small.

> A leadership mentee raised by a my-way-or-the-highway father who believed that a particular management style was somehow in his DNA. He bristled at this layer of rock but didn't know how to dismantle it (and didn't dare change, for fear of appearing weak). He continued to execute an outdated, overbearing leadership style and feel shame and regret about it until he finally worked up the courage to ask for help finding a different way.

> A colleague who got her heart broken by a shitty ex-husband—and took away from that experience that she was unlovable. Everyone experiences rejection—sometimes the most cruel and merciless kinds—but when it translates to a

layer of self-deprecation and insecurity, it becomes particularly stubborn rock.

> A client who believed, deep down, that nothing could ever undo the fact that he defined himself not by his successes, his actions, or his relationships, but by his obesity. The legacy of being bullied as a child had him encased in mountains of rock. That burden kept him from even dreaming that on any level he might be a masterpiece in the making.

I've had the privilege of working with each of these individuals, seeing them grow and change and begin to get free of their feelings of inadequacy and self-doubt. This last client is one who's been part of my life for a year at this writing. He's put in a tremendous amount of work to get free of his demoralizing self-view. Over a period of twelve months, he dedicated himself to freeing his best self instead of hiding his worst. With that perspective, he took up walking, then running. He lost weight. He started writing a book. He got promoted at work. He fell more deeply in love with his wife. And he gained a level of confidence that was unfathomable when we first met.

Often, when we get together, this man thanks me for helping him make these changes, but I promise you, I didn't do *any* of it. My role in this relationship is nothing more than asking questions and listening to answers. I aspired to help this extraordinary person recognize how much he was being constricted by layer upon layer of rock. I can't chisel anyone else's burdens away, but sometimes I can lay a pickaxe at their feet. After a while, this man decided to pick his up. He used the mental SHIFTs that follow (and many more) to put it to work. And since he started chiseling, there's been no stopping him. The man is crushing it, writing a story in which he *finally* gets to be the lead.

SHIFT #1: STOP ASKING PERMISSION

Notice what all the scenarios above have in common?

They all start with the actions of someone other than the hero of the story. The mean teacher, the hostile boss, the overbearing father, the cruel ex, the bullying peers—they're all front and center, laying the rock that binds us. That was certainly the case in my own life. Even before I started school, I was convinced that being unwanted by my father was my defining characteristic.

Truth is, at the root of almost every example of rock building up around us, there's a victim story. Sometimes we don't notice it's there. We may not overtly blame anybody. We just add up our issues and decide we are limited because of certain circumstances or people.

One essential step in chiseling toward your highest form is stepping out of that mindset. That process begins when you stop asking permission—to be who you want, to pursue goals of your choosing, to succeed or fail on your own terms, to focus on betterment instead of achievement, and to be unapologetically selfish about taking care of yourself. Nobody gets to dictate your life, your growth, your success.

In a victim mindset, we're basically (and constantly) asking others if it's okay to be successful. In personal relationships you may wonder: *When are my friends going to start supporting me? When is my spouse going to understand me? When is my mom going to respect me? When is my friend going to start going to the gym with me?*

In our professional lives, the questions can be equally limiting: *When is my boss going to trust me? When is my colleague going to give me the credit I deserve? When is the government going to lower interest rates so I can sell more? When is the company going to change these oppressive rules?*

Those are all *victim* questions. They put the asker at the mercy of someone else. And the sad truth about putting yourself in that position is that it keeps you exactly where you are—always waiting for change and growth and good things to come to you. Always buried under a lifetime's worth of accumulated rock.

My life was defined by questions like these for years. Maybe you know the feeling. My failures and limitations were never about me. Life was about what was happening *to* me; what people were doing *to* me; how the world was keeping me down.

I was lucky to start doubting this mindset in my midtwenties when I met the woman who is now my wife. Talking with her, I couldn't help but notice she was framing the world with a different kind of question. Instead of *Why is this happening to me?* she'd ask *What can I learn from this?* Instead of *When is so-and-so going to help?* she'd ask *How can I take charge?* Instead of *How can I possibly tackle all of this?* she'd ask *What matters most to me?* And then she'd roll up her sleeves and get started.

Her questions were *victor* questions. And I'm telling you, they were a revelation for me. Getting to know this woman's strength and spirit gave me my first glimpse at how different life is when you wake up every morning and plot your course in terms of what you will learn, what you can accomplish, and how great you can be.

At Cannonball Moments, when we say that the quality of your life is predicated on the questions you ask yourself, this dialogue is at the center of our intention. My coaching clients know that if they start a conversation by blaming or crediting circumstances, we're gonna start over again. When you put your focus on the state of the economy, on the competition, on the tyranny of the overfull calendar, on what the other guy is doing—you're asking: *When can I be successful? When is it my turn?* You are asking permission and focusing on all the elements of the equation that are not yours to control. If you keep telling yourself outside factors are determining your path, then they will.

I challenge you to approach your days and your hardships remembering that your life is a masterpiece in the making. In that story, you are fundamentally capable of greatness and joy and the experience of abundance. In that mindset, you don't have to blame or beg or wait or whine. You choose to control what you can. You learn and grow and get better.

When you make that shift, you step into your power. The more comfortable you become exercising it, the easier you'll find the process of freeing yourself from layer after layer of narrative rock.

SHIFT #2: FIND YOUR PRIDE

Recently a friend confided in me that she was struggling. I asked what was going on, and she explained how she'd been feeling unmotivated and "kind of empty."

"But I'm working my way through it," she said. "I'm keeping a gratitude journal."

"That's great," I replied. "But it might not work."

She looked at me like I'd lost my mind. Because, I mean, who doesn't acknowledge the healing powers of gratitude?

I scrambled to explain myself: I *love* gratitude. I *live* gratitude. I acknowledge gratitude as an essential component of strength, empathy, and joy. There may be no more effective means of moving toward happiness than feeling grateful.

But gratitude is not a cure-all; it's not the duct tape of emotions. And it can especially come up short when what you're seeking is *motivation*—the drive to get up and go *do* something.

For that, you need a healthy dose of pride.

At this point my friend laughed out loud. *Pride? As in the seven deadly sins? Seriously?*

I asked her to hear me out. These two emotions—always-a-gold-star gratitude and isn't-that-a-sin pride—are both priceless assets.

Here's why: When you work from gratitude, you almost always default to appreciating external entities. Ask anyone you know to name ten things they're grateful for and see what they say. We are grateful for families, friends, homes, careers, pets, faith communities, vacations, flowers, fresh bread, falling snow, date nights—the list goes on and on. But how many of those things can we point to and say: *I did that?* Few to none. Because of that, it's possible to be incredibly grateful and *still* struggle with feeling flawed or unproductive or defeated.

Just as gratitude tends to be an outward-looking experience, pride is one that looks within. Pride is internal—the way you feel about what you are or did—and it is your single greatest intrinsic source of motivation. If you do something and feel good about it, you'll want to do more. It's a simple concept—if you can allow yourself to feel an emotion that has a checkered reputation.

Over the years I've asked many coaching clients to write about their gratitude, and they've almost universally engaged in that process and found it easy—even when times are hard.

But when I ask clients to start a pride journal, first they resist. Then they struggle to execute. They find it difficult, even painful, to acknowledge even an ounce of pride.

I struggled with this for a long time, working to extricate ego, which is the idea of being *better* than anyone else, from *pride*, the idea that something I've done matters or is effective or makes me feel good about myself. There is an essential difference. After my trip to Florence, I was able to finally make peace with it, because I was able to believe that deep within me there's a core that is exactly right. I didn't make it. I can't destroy it. But I can put it to good use and feel positive and hopeful and, yes, proud of that.

In any quest to gain freedom from the layers of rock that have built up around you, pride is one of your most effective tools. When one of my clients gets out of bed at five o'clock each morning and walks two miles, that's a source of pride. That pride is enough to ensure he'll do it again the next day. When a struggling leader makes a generous, honest gesture that connects with an employee, she goes home feeling good about herself—and that's going to make the next generous, honest gesture easier to give.

I do recommend keeping a gratitude journal or whiteboard or memo on your phone. But right alongside it, try keeping a pride journal, too. Each list deserves a new entry every day. See the best in the world and the best in yourself. If you can do that, then your growth and greatness possibilities become infinite.

> *Pride is internal—the way you feel about what you are or did—and it is your single greatest intrinsic source of motivation. If you do something and feel good about it, you'll want to do more. It's a simple concept—if you can allow yourself to feel an emotion that has a checkered reputation.*

SHIFT #3: RISK A LITTLE EXPOSURE

There's a piece of this puzzle that's easy to forget—one that's a seminal reason many people choose to stay encased in limitations and negativity and victim mindsets. Truth is, there's an upside to staying covered up by the narratives that create all that rock: Being tucked up inside a lifetime of accumulated layers can feel *safe*. Accepting stories that lay our limitations and failings on other people and extenuating circumstances can be surprisingly comfortable. All those layers of rock can feel like a shell—one you burrow into when you're feeling insecure or fearful or angry or insignificant.

But the *David*? The work of art that was always there in the stone? The statue is literally naked. The guy is spectacular—but also utterly exposed to scrutiny.

There's a trade-off that gradually takes place when you start dealing with the narratives you've accumulated, the ones that keep you from stretching and growing. As you let go of the burden and the false sense of security the layers of rock provide, you'll learn to be more secure in your deep-down worth—even at times when you're a little less secure in your position.

Whatever spectacular masterpiece lies within you, you're going to have to face some exposure to find it.

I've thought about this for years—before, during, and after the day I spent in Florence. If I could give my twenty-five-year-old self any advice, I'd start with this: *Your path is going to be plagued with rejection and self-doubt, failure and misery. Eighty percent of your early years are going to feel like they're comprised of hardship. You are going to suffer.*

Tough love, right? But it's not the whole story. It's not even the important part. That part is the other 20 percent—the portion of this life where that guy finds his way to a loving marriage, to amazing kids, to having a professional impact beyond his wildest dreams.

Even though the path to that great life *demands* shaking off rock and feeling exposed and vulnerable and sometimes beaten down, I'd put my arm around my younger and far more foolish self and tell him, without hesitation: *Start anyway. Start today. Face the adversity and endure the pain. Because along the way you're going to know joy and pride you earned by your struggle, and more love and gratitude and even wisdom than you know how to carry. And you're going to weave it all into the story of a well-lived life.*

Or, you know, you can just keep doing what you're doing: punching a clock, sitting on a barstool, keeping people at arm's length, staying "safe" under your pile of rock . . .

SHIFT #4: FOLLOW YOUR EPIPHANIES

I don't pretend to understand the origins of thought processes or the way the universe brings mysteries and inspiration to my door. But I do know it happens all the time that an idea comes, or sticks, and something in the sentiment begs for more attention. In my early life, I'd discard those moments of possibility and clarity as out of my reach or out of the realm of possibility. Fleeting thoughts like *Maybe I should try college;* or *Maybe it's not in my best interest to hang out with this crowd;* or *Maybe I could find a career path that feels fulfilling instead of just having one that pays the bills.* But every time, my critical, victim-oriented brain would jump in and answer: *No way. That's outside your comfort zone. That's not possible FOR YOU.*

But after your self-view shifts, after you refute the idea that you have something to hide, after you break out from under your heavy layers of rock—then you can listen with an open mind. You can give credit to mental nudges that strike a chord—the kind of nudge that could be called an epiphany. You may even come to believe, as I have for a long time now, that an epiphany is an inner belief starting to shine through. It's your best self trying to get out.

With that mindset, when you think about a new possibility, you don't have to shut it down with negativity and automatic challenges. Instead, you can sit with it. You can allow yourself to be curious, to wonder: *What does it mean? How would I do it? What would it help me accomplish? What's driving me to consider this?*

In the past, I always defaulted to saying *I can't.* Now, I approach new ideas with an open mind. I question, sure—but I don't lead with doubt.

Ditto for those moments when I have a sensory experience and think it's a sign. I don't ignore them. I respect them enough to give them a little of my time.

For me, this book is a perfect example of this process in action. It was a dream of mine for at least a decade to write—to fully explore the concepts and practices that are in these pages alongside my own story.

It easily could have not happened. Writing a book is a long, painstaking, expensive, and sometimes frustrating process. I've got a family to love and support, a company to run, keynotes to give, coaching clients to visit and encourage and question. Years went by when the idea of a book was just a distant mirage.

And then one night I landed in Chicago in the wee hours and called for an Uber. The terminal was wide-open and empty—so empty I snapped a picture as I made my way to the exits to help me remember it that way.

I figured I'd be waiting a long time for a car at two o'clock in the morning, but my ride was already there when I reached the door.

The driver looked to be around sixty and spoke with a thick accent I couldn't place. As we departed the airport and set out on the ninety-minute ride to my hotel in the suburbs, it quickly became apparent that the man was at least as much a philosopher as he was a driver. We cruised along the eerily deserted highways, and he launched into one heavy conversational topic after another. Faith. Fate. Purpose. Love. Death. He'd ask a question, wait for an answer, share an opinion, sit quietly for a moment, and then ask another. At no time in the conversation did I tell this man what I do for a living, but when we were a few minutes from my hotel, he ended one of his pauses with the question, "What are you speaking about tomorrow?"

I'd been getting groggy, but in that moment I snapped awake.

"How do you know I'm speaking tomorrow?"

Instead of explaining, he waved his hand like that was an irrelevant question and said, "You're going to give a powerful speech. It's going to be excellent."

I didn't know what else to say, and he went back to his between-question mode of peaceable silence. There was nothing vaguely hostile or negative in the moment. If anything, he'd sounded encouraging, reassuring, even paternal.

When we arrived at my hotel, the lobby was dark. I hopped out of the car and tried the door.

Locked.

I rang the bell, hoping there was an attendant on duty. When I walked back to the car for my bag, the driver got out and stood beside me, apparently intent on waiting until this was resolved. We both eyed the darkened door, which mercifully opened after a couple minutes. When it did, the driver turned to me, shook my hand, and said, "Good luck to you."

As he was walking away, he turned back and said, clear as day, "And you know, it's probably time you write the book."

What was I supposed to do with that? I remember standing there, watching him get behind the wheel and drive away, thinking, *What* the hell *just happened?*

And then, a heartbeat later, wondering, *Was that* God?

I can still picture that moment, every detail of it. And what I remember most is that I felt an internal SHIFT. My entire adult life I'd been considering the reasons why I could not pursue this dream. And in that moment it went from an unlikely aspiration to a future certainty.

This was an epiphany facilitated by a mysterious stranger, in an unfamiliar city, in the middle of the night, when I was punch-drunk tired and not the least bit looking for a revelation. I could have shaken it off. Forgotten it. Convinced myself I didn't hear his words.

But this was the version of me who had seen the *David*. I was actively cultivating new faith in my worth and capability. So I took the whole weird, wonderful encounter and wrapped my arms around it. And from then on when I thought about writing a book, my mind was spinning logistics. *How do I? When can I? What do I do first?*

> This was an epiphany facilitated by a mysterious stranger, in an unfamiliar city, in the middle of the night, when I was punch-drunk tired and not the least bit looking for a revelation. I could have shaken it off. Forgotten it. Convinced myself I didn't hear his words.
>
> But I'd seen the David. I was cultivating new faith in my worth and capability. So I took the whole weird, wonderful encounter and wrapped my arms around it.

SHIFT #5: REMEMBER THE ENDGAME

In 2011 an Australian palliative care worker named Bronnie Ware published her book *The Top Five Regrets of the Dying*—a title that went on to connect with a million readers. For several years, Ware took care of patients who were in their last weeks of life. Seeking meaning and purpose in her own story, she found it both in the work she was doing and in the observations it afforded her. And she vowed to learn from the regrets her patients expressed.

When Ware wrote about her experience, she gave voice to insights many of us feel but fail to name. The first regret she shares is especially poignant, rolled up in the story of an elderly woman who wanted nothing more than to get out from under the thumb of an overbearing husband—but never did. In her last days, she said, "I wish I'd had the courage to live a life true to myself, not the life others expected of me."

You have to wonder how the other four regrets can compete, because this feels like a universal and eternal worry. It's certainly one that deserves attention long before the last months of any life.

The biggest change I see in my clients who begin to plot their lives around freeing their masterpiece instead of around covering up all the ways they think they're flawed is that the gnawing regrets that lead to this kind of sentiment edge away. I don't believe there's any balm that wipes out all remorse, but trusting that you are good and worthy at your core goes a long way toward easing fears of exposure and failure and rejection. It's the ultimate *I'm okay; you're okay*, because it allows you to believe you're *already* great. You're just working on bringing some of that greatness to the surface.

QUESTIONS
TO CONSIDER

> How much of your time are you devoting to hiding, crushing, and compensating for flaws? Are you open to a fundamental change to a mindset in which you're freeing your best self instead of burying a broken one? If you have a faith, that can likely help. After all, would your creator design you to be broken?

  – Over the years I've often struggled with this and come back time and again to a basic truth: If I'm truly a person of faith, then my life's work is not overcoming any deficit. It's finding my purpose, exploring my potential, and embracing the strengths and gifts within me.

> Are you waiting for permission to be great? To try something new? Do you keep telling yourself that if/when some outside factor changes, then you'll make your move? Go to the gym? Do something romantic for your partner? Do something fun and spontaneous with your kids? Take that first step to starting your own business? If so, how can you reframe your approach and put yourself in the driver's seat? What one step can you take right now to start exploring that possibility?

> Do you need to make peace with pride before you can welcome it into your life? If so, try taking it as a separate entity from ego and arrogance. They are not the same. True pride is not about comparison; it's about effort and excellence. How can you find a little of that in every day? And how will you acknowledge it?

> When has it felt like the universe was tapping you on the shoulder and trying to get you a message? Are you listening? Could you ask a few questions, open a door to possibility? I'm the first to admit my Chicago Uber driver story is a strange one, but I bet you have a strange story of your own. Sometimes the missing piece that will facilitate your next big leap forward is right there on the periphery of your life, waiting to be acknowledged.

> How can you help the people in your life keep from adding layers of narrative rock to themselves and their stories?

Can you offer genuine praise? Can you show them it's okay to feel pride, to use it as a motivator? Can you show gratitude? Can you counter a negative story with a positive one? You can't chip away at anyone else's edges, but you can help them feel safe and loved and respected when they set out to do it themselves.

• CANNONBALL BOOK CLUB FAVORITES •

A Return to Love

Marianne Williamson

CHAD'S NOTE: I coached girls' basketball for many years, and in that time I gave a copy of a quote from this book to every one of my players. I have Williamson's words framed on the wall of my office, too. Her book is deeply empowering and eloquently reassuring that we all have greatness within us. I return to it not only for encouragement to go big and be true to myself, but also because I know when I do those things, I liberate my daughters to do the same.

Our deepest fear is not that we are inadequate. Our deepest fear is that we are powerful beyond measure. It is our light, not our darkness, that most frightens us. We ask ourselves, "Who am I to be brilliant, gorgeous, talented, fabulous?" Actually, who are you not to be? You are a child of God. Your playing small does not serve the world.

David and Goliath: Underdogs, Misfits, and the Art of Battling Giants

Malcolm Gladwell

CHAD'S NOTE: Gladwell has become the gold standard author of eye-opening books, and of all his titles, this is the one I come back to time and again. It allowed me to learn more about a story that has great resonance in my own life. It changed my understanding of courage. It is an essential look at going against the odds and trusting that you are worthy of winning.

You see the giant and the shepherd in the Valley of Elah and your eye is drawn to the man with sword and shield and the glittering armor. But so much of what is beautiful and valuable in the world comes from the shepherd, who has more strength and purpose than we ever imagine.

7

STRUCTURE SUCCESS

Is the structure of your days shaping your story?

Do your habits and patterns drag you down or help you rise?

Every story has structure. Not just the epic arc that takes you from birth to death, but a million smaller narratives as well. They're as big as a childhood or a career; as formal and ritual as a wedding or a funeral; as small but indelible as an ocean-side afternoon when you helped your kids build sandcastles and then watched waves wash those castles away. Every year, every week, every day—each is part of your story. Taken together they're the whole saga of your life.

What does structure have to do with it? Structure enompasses the schedules and habits, rhythms and patterns on which we hang our choices and actions. It's how we get from morning to night. It's how we let ideas and activities flow from one to the next. It dictates how we plan, how we follow through, how we function, and, often, how we feel.

And we've got structure in place for just about everything. A few examples:

> *When the alarm goes off: I hit snooze three times; or I bound out of bed; or I kiss my spouse good morning; or I take a big news-and-email hit off my phone that feels like my oxygen . . .*

> *When I'm happy: I listen to music; or I mix a cocktail; or I write down why; or I play with my dog . . .*

> *When I'm frustrated: I shout at my family; or I take a walk; or I eat my feelings; or I call my brother/friend/mom and talk it through . . .*

> *When I have a free hour: I read a book; or I rest my eyes; or I hit the gym; or I get outside; or I have a standing date with Netflix . . .*

Even when we're not thinking about them, the go-to structures we create shape our realities. Like guardrails (or fences), they keep us in familiar territory and make our days predictable. Not necessarily a bad thing—*unless* those structures don't align with either our self-view or our aspirations. When that happens, this nuts-and-bolts side of life can easily keep us stuck in lifestyles that aren't the ones we want. It's exactly this trap that leads people to wake up one morning and wonder where the last ten or twenty years went.

Just like almost everything else in which we have free will, the structures we create are directly tied to the stories we tell ourselves.

If you keep telling yourself you can't possibly make time for that class you've been wanting to take, for example, you'll stick with the schedules and habits that make that true.

If you keep telling yourself that 9 AM meeting you despise every day is a nonnegotiable, it'll continue to bog you down.

If you keep telling yourself those hours in front of the television or doomscrolling are the only way you can relax, you'll never get around to finding a better option.

Every time you tell yourself those stories, and every time you lean into the structures that support them, you're sowing the limitations they create a little deeper in your brain. And the brain *loves* routine, loves not having to sweat what's going to happen next. In a study done at Queen's University in Canada, researchers found that a staggering *95 percent* of our thoughts are repeats—just the same things that crossed your mind a minute ago or an hour ago or yesterday. And the vast majority of those thoughts are *negative*. It's an evolution thing—designed to keep you always mindful of danger.

But if you're not in danger, if you're looking to learn and grow and change and live the richest, most rewarding life possible—then you can be deliberate in establishing new stories, an upgraded self-view, and new structures in your life that support positive change.

Even when we're not thinking about them, the go-to structures we create shape our realities. Like guardrails (or fences), they keep us in familiar territory and make our days predictable. Not necessarily a bad thing—unless those structures don't align with either our self-view or our aspirations.

RUNNING MAN

My own best example of a life-altering habit change comes in the form of the love affair with running I embarked on in my midforties. Several years ago, during a speaking engagement in Portugal, I said, just offhand, not even reading from my notes, *"I could run a marathon* if I had the right mindset and the right self-view."

In the moment, it sounded great. And so true! No matter that I hadn't run a hundred yards in more than twenty years. It sounded so great, in fact, that on the long flight home, I decided I was going to do it. By the time we touched down in Baltimore, I'd applied for a lottery spot to run the New York City Marathon.

Then I forgot about it and moved on with my busy life.

A few weeks later I was working in Texas, and I stopped at a gas station to check messages. At the top of my inbox? An email from the New York Road Runners association. The first line—the one you can see in the preview window before you open the file—announced, *"Congratulations! You have won the opportunity to run . . ."*

I can't win a scratch off. I can't win a raffle. But I won a slot to run 26.2 miles.

Woo-hoo??

In all honesty, I looked around that parking lot for a few seconds, checking for witnesses, thinking: *If I delete this now, nobody has to know.* And then I did the exact opposite. I posted it on Facebook—and in doing so made a commitment to follow through.

What did I know about long-distance running? Not a damned thing except that I wanted to prove I could do it. Also that I'd really like to have a New York City Marathon medal hanging in my office.

I hired a coach—one who strongly advised me to train for a shorter race and work up to running a marathon the following year. When I refused (repeatedly), he went ahead and gave me my first assignment: "Run one mile."

Oh man, I was so sure he was underestimating me. I told him I could do more.

He said, "Just one mile."

"But I've got new shoes. I can do more!"

"Chad. Run a mile."

Brimming with confidence and energy, I said, "Okay, I'll call you in a few minutes when I get back," and headed out the door.

I live at the top of a hillside cul-de-sac with just a few houses, so I trotted down the driveway toward the connecting street. By the time I got to the bottom of the loop, my lungs were on fire. I chalked it up to not being sufficiently warmed up and kept running. At the half-mile point, my legs started to cramp and my heart was slamming against the walls of my chest. I pushed onward, certain I'd loosen up and ease past the strain.

No such luck.

When I hit the mile mark, I collapsed by the side of the road, gasping and aching and cramping in muscles I'd forgotten I even had. I was wrecked. Sadly, since I hadn't been smart enough to run a half mile out and a half mile back, I had to call my wife and ask if she could please come get me and drive me home.

Day one, mile one was all about pain and humiliation.

This was the way I trained—in the manner of a man who wants to be able to *say* he ran a marathon but doesn't care about actually becoming a runner.

In November of 2016, I lined up on the Verrazzano Bridge for the race, feeling nervous, scared, sick to my stomach—but determined to get through. I'd run a grand total of 213 miles in training—meaning I'd skipped many more miles than I'd taken. My prep work should have been hundreds of miles more.

My lack of preparation showed. I ran and panted. Cramped and cried. Prayed for mercy. At the twenty-mile mark I was ready to tap out, then I spied my family up ahead on the sidewalk. My wife, my girls, my brother—all cheering me on. Kim must have known I was ready to call it, because when she locked eyes with me, the only thing she said was "Look at your wrist."

I wear a rubber bracelet that says *I AM ENOUGH*. I'd been wearing one for years, since not long after our trip to Florence to see the *David*. It is a tool that kicks off a kind of word-association power boost in me every time I look at it. That day in New York, even in my physically and emotionally drained state, I looked from my wife to my wrist and pictured the familiar words tumbling through my head. I AM. WORTHY. ENOUGH. GRATEFUL. BLESSED. A MASTERPIECE.

I sucked air to the very bottom of my lungs, fixed my eyes ahead, and kept moving.

In the end, in the dark, I gutted out a finish. For reference, the qualifying time for an eighty-year-old man looking to run the race that year was a full hour less than my six-hour run. But for me, getting across the line was a matter of willpower and ego, and I *propelled* myself to the end.

When the race was over, the back of my family's SUV became a makeshift ambulance. I crawled in there on my hands and knees and groaned, ravaged from the effort. To be honest, I thought it might become a hearse before I got home. I'd never been in so much physical pain in my life—and of course it only got worse the next day.

I did get my medal. But I didn't change for the better. If anything, I felt an old familiar and unwelcome feeling about the race—that sense that I'd failed to rise to my capability.

I needed to understand where I'd gone wrong (besides the obvious training shortcomings). I wanted to be better.

The answer boiled down to two factors: my self-view and the way I'd structured my training around that view. I'd been telling myself I wanted to check an achievement off a list. The gist of that story was pretty limiting: *Chad crosses the finish line and earns his medal. The end.*

But if I truly wanted to embody everything running a marathon meant to me—physical strength, endurance, commitment, discipline, vigorous health, a level of excellence—then I'd have to tell an entirely different story. I'd need to shift my self-view and decide: *I AM a runner. I AM an athlete.* I'd need a more robust structure. A structure that empowered me to put in the work.

I sat with that for a while and then committed to doing it all again, but better. I committed to changing the narrative—a process that saw me improve in the 2017 NY Marathon and truly come into my own two years after my first race.

In 2018, when I lined up on the bridge and waited for the sound of the starting gun, I wasn't scared. I wasn't anxious. I wasn't disappointed in myself over the way I'd prepared. I gazed out over New York Harbor and felt a sense of profound gratitude and, despite the excitement buzzing all around me, deep peace. I'd run 1,158 training miles over the course that year. I was lean, strong, rested, and well nourished.

And I knew that no matter what happened over the 26.2 miles ahead, I'd already won.

What does it take to get from a "beta" marathon—full of mistakes and buggy as hell—to one that's satisfying beyond words? It's the same X factor that gets you from dreaming about starting a company to hanging its sign over a new door. The same thing that gets you from being a struggling entry-level sales rep to being the team's number one. The same thing that gets you from wishing you had a better relationship with your family to bonding with them in one meaningful way after another.

It takes seeing your capability and choosing not to settle for less—then weaving every ounce of your conviction into the structures of your stories and days to make it all line up.

The tools you use will be unique to you—whether it's a monitored system or a coach, a class or an accountability plan, installing software or enlisting a companion. No matter what you choose, though, there are a handful of structuring principles that are universally useful in making this happen. Let's look at five of the most effective: shaking things up, giving yourself permission, defining expectations, getting real about time, and embracing process over outcome.

What does it take to get from a "beta" marathon—full of mistakes and buggy as hell—to one that's satisfying beyond words? It takes seeing your capability and choosing not to settle for less—then weaving every ounce of your conviction into the structures of your stories and days to make it all line up.

STRUCTURING PRINCIPLE #1: SHAKE THINGS UP

Perhaps the most miraculous thing about the human mind is that it is endlessly changeable and upgradeable. We're all capable of reframing perspectives and then creating habits (mental *and* physical) that support those new versions. We can always learn more, absorb more, engage more. That ability, that *neuroplasticity*, is the reason somebody like Tony Robbins can make the transition from being a part-time janitor to the most sought-after executive coach on the planet. The reason a "slow student" like Albert Einstein can develop into one of the greatest scientific minds of a generation. The reason an intern can make it all the way to the corner office. And yes, also the reason a middle-aged guy like me can evolve from a runner who had nothing but grit going for me to one who finds inspiration and satisfaction in every day's training trek.

If we want to get better and grow, we can't allow bare-minimum routines and habits to put us on autopilot. We can't settle into the ho-hum. If the structure of your days has gotten to feel a little too rote, if you're in a rut, the first step in shaking things up is putting your powerful, creative brain back to work.

It all starts with doing something, anything new. New story. New place. New route to the office. New food. New habits. A new friend. Pushing yourself in any new way.

Here's what happens when you do something new: You light up an entirely different part of your brain from the ones that manage all the normal, same-as-yesterday business. Your brain gets a call to attention. Suddenly your senses are engaged. You're thinking about what happens next—and that is the perfect time to start changing a habit.

My favorite way to understand how this works goes back to a psychology concept from the 1960s called *eustress*. If you think of your comfort zone—the place where all your repetitive thoughts and no-brainer routines take place—as a big circle, then eustress is a narrow range outside the margins of that zone. It's not an entirely comfortable state of mind, but it's not the freak-out, hair-on-fire territory of *distress* either. By definition, eustress is a positive cognitive state that challenges you. It's the state in which you learn, discover, make connections, gain perspective, and grow.

And you just can't get there if you stick to the same routines, habits, meals, sights, people, places, and thoughts over and over again.

This has become such a fundamental concept for me that I am constantly putting my toe over the line—out of my comfort zone and into something new. Shaking things up has in some ways *become* one of my core habits. I started a podcast, for example, because it gave me the opportunity to meet new and fascinating people—and to start conversations I never would have found within my circle. I read constantly because I crave new ideas. I embrace new physical challenges—throwing myself into new workouts and running experiences.

Often, these steps aren't about the outcome. They're about the great energy, excitement, and openness I feel when I do each of them. They're about getting into that state of learning and growth.

The truth is, every new facet you introduce into your life opens a window to restructure how you expend your time and energy.

It's a spark you can use to light a new path, to fuel an idea, or even to burn down routines and habits that are holding you back.

It doesn't have to be big. Take a day off and do something you've never done before. Try a new cuisine. Go to a concert or a lecture. Get up in time to watch a sunrise. Change the route of your commute.

Shaking up your routine provides perspective—one big step away from the habits and routines that may be holding you back.

STRUCTURING PRINCIPLE #2: GIVE YOURSELF PERMISSION

Many of the giant structural blocks between us and our objectives are self-imposed. We deny ourselves the privilege of trying new things (or getting back to old ones we find satisfying). We deny ourselves big swings that might lead to failures. We deny ourselves time. We deny ourselves priority.

Nothing changes until this denial stops. Until you give yourself permission to pursue whatever is most important to you. Getting over the hump can be made a little easier with the advice that thought leader Jim Collins shared in his bestselling management book *Built to Last*. Collins wrote about what he called "the tyranny of the *OR*." The essence of his argument is one I put into practice almost every day: a trust that we don't have to pit our options *against* one another. We don't always have to choose. Not every choice has to be about sacrifice. It is possible to embrace multiple priorities and excel at them. It's possible to find compromises that work, to focus on *and* instead of *or*.

I firmly believe that none of us is created to have just one thing or another—one joy, one relationship, one priority. Our minds are capable of learning and growth. Our bodies are designed to adapt and respond to our efforts. When we push ourselves a little bit, we often discover we're just scratching the surface of our capability.

In my own life, I've seen this in action many times—including the evolution of a body that basically said *heck no* when I ran my first mile to one that's conditioned to accomplish a fifty-mile race just a few years later.

But before you can make a change, you have to give yourself permission to try—to stretch. When the stories we embrace for ourselves get bigger, it becomes easier to change our schedules and habits to match.

Of course, none of us lives in a vacuum. We've got people to whom we're accountable. And sometimes giving yourself permission to try something new opens the door to friction—with families, employers and employees, coworkers, and friends. It's a logical shift, because other people's thoughts are mostly repetitive, too. When you make a change that impacts your kids' or your spouse's or your office mate's routine, then they've got to adjust and make changes just like you do.

That's when it's time to take all those expectations you set for yourself and sit down to negotiate shared expectations with someone else.

Most people don't initiate this process until things are far gone. In fact, I often meet with new coaching clients who are at their wits' end. They are doing amazing things, but they're overwhelmed and unhappy.

That was the case for an executive I work with and tremendously admire, who I'll call Rose. Rose is an amazing leader in her profession—smart, funny, strong, kind—and she carries herself with an energy that can't be taught. Employees and colleagues want to be around her. They want to do good work for her.

Privately, though, Rose struggles to believe she is important, that she is the hero of her story. She's dealt with insecurities, and she's spent an awful lot of time trying to "fix" herself. To that end, she takes on far more than her fair share of any and every task. She works, she leads and mentors, she's a committee chair for her church, she cooks and cleans, she walks the dog, she helps her kids with homework, she serves on the neighborhood watch, and so much more.

It'd be great if all those things fit into the structure of Rose's life, but they absolutely do not. She goes and goes and goes, constantly trying to pour more of her time and energy from an empty cup. And then one day when we sat down together to talk about how things were going, Rose put her cards on the table. She was drained. Unhappy. Failing on multiple fronts. She has a partner and a family and friends and a big corporate team, but instead of feeling blessed by those relationships, she felt obligated to meet her invisible metrics for each of them, all the time.

Her words: "It's all so joyless."

When I asked what steps she could take to ease some of the pressure she was feeling, Rose's answer sounded hopeless.

"There aren't enough hours," she said. "I can't keep up. I don't even feel like I'm *living*. I just do all the tasks I've been programmed to do."

Pressed about what she'd do if she had all the time and money in the world, she said, "Well, I'd go for a walk every morning—a leisurely walk, not a beat-the-clock walk. I'd take the weekend sometimes and go away by myself. I'd read, for fun, without being interrupted or feeling guilty about it."

And then, with her voice a little wistful, she said, "I might take a tennis lesson."

This seemed like a low bar as far as expectations go. We should all have sufficient freedom to be able to take one tennis lesson. But Rose was adamant that the demands of her life wouldn't allow any of it. She'd tried. It'd been a bust. The kids didn't have dinner. Her husband was cranky. Her son failed to turn in a homework assignment. A day off from work meant a week of catching up on all she'd missed.

I asked about her kids, and she told me she had three: two boys and a girl. Her boys were in their early teens and her daughter, Jen, was nine.

"And how long are you going to wait before you have the talk with her?" I wondered.

"What talk?"

"You know," I said, "where you explain how life works? Where you say, 'Jen, right now you're nine, and you're happy. It's all about you! It's going to stay that way for a while, probably until you finish college. But after that, you'll start a career. You may fall in love and maybe start a family. Once those things happen, your life will need to be about sacrifices. You're going to have to give up most of the things that give you joy and a sense of accomplishment and peace. You'll have to *trade* them for your career and a family. That's just the way life works.'

"At what age are you going to have that talk with your daughter?"

Rose stared at me, and I wasn't sure if she was going to burst into tears or explode with anger.

The tears won.

When I asked why she was upset, she said, "I'd never have that conversation with my daughter. Not with anybody."

And then she said, without a hint of irony, "Because no one should have to live their life like that."

"Then why are you?" I asked. "At what point did you decide that you were no longer worthy of the life you want?"

She shook her head, said, "I don't know."

I said, "You know when it's going to stop, right? When you give yourself permission to have joy and outside engagement and personal fulfillment again. When you choose to be unapologetically selfish."

That day, we put our heads together to strategize what the utterly necessary shifts in Rose's life might look like. We scoured her calendar, studying the allocation of her time and asking of each slot: *Is this working?* This was not an easy exercise (and it was one that would be ongoing long after that first day), but it was an important first step. Rose identified areas where she wanted to cut back. She flagged hours that were disproportionately burning her energy and making her miserable. She considered how a transition to a more inward-focused life would change things for her family, her coworkers, and other people who were part of her community.

Rose's next step was to have a different, equally important talk with her family (and then with her colleagues). It wasn't the conversation we'd discussed—not a conversation of defeat. It was a strong, powerful woman's first act in reclaiming some autonomy and flexibility in her life.

Next time we spoke, she couldn't wait to tell me how it had gone. Rose had sat down with her family and said, "I've been failing you, because I've been teaching you by my own actions to put yourselves last. I've discouraged you from speaking up about what you need. I've shown you a lot of sacrifice, but not nearly enough joy and independence. That's not what I want for you—and it's not what I want for me. So I'm going to make some changes. I'm going to exercise. I'm going to read. I'm going to take one weekend every couple months and spend time doing something that's fun for me. I want you to know I'm doing these things not in spite of you but because of you. I'm going to get healthier and happier, and I want you to think about what *you* need to be healthier and happier, too."

And then she actually did it. After giving herself permission to deal with a problem that had been festering and growing for years, Rose revamped her schedule and stopped spending every minute of her day working on other people's priorities. She's been feeling stronger and more capable ever since.

The truth is, every one of us is worthy of an amazing, fulfilling life. But until you give yourself permission to explore what that looks like for you, you won't find it.

STRUCTURING PRINCIPLE #3: DEFINE EXPECTATIONS

At a conference in Las Vegas, I spoke to a crowd of executives, all in town for their industry's biggest conference. It'd been a long week of meetings and presentations, keynotes and cocktail hours—not to mention a fair bit of gambling in the off hours.

We were in the room to talk about leadership, and I asked if, by a show of hands, these CEOs, VPs, and directors could tell me who among them does a great job of defining expectations for their employees. Dozens of hands went up.

"Great," I said, as my colleague handed out notecards and pencils. "I'd like everyone with their hand up to write down on a notecard the three biggest expectations you have of your employees."

We waited a few minutes for this to happen, and then I set a stack of hundred-dollar bills on the podium.

"In the spirit of Vegas, I'd like to propose a bet," I said. "I'd like to call each of your offices and ask whoever answers the phone if they can tell me the three biggest expectations the company has of them. First one to match up with what you wrote down wins. It should be easy money, right?"

Hands around the room went down.

Because it's not that easy. It's not easy to set clear expectations for yourself or for anybody else—most notably because most expectations are set *unconsciously*. Like those stories that build up around us, they just happen, so gradually and subtly that we often fail to notice it's happening—let alone when some of those expectations are problematic or even flat-out unrealistic.

A rudimentary example: I'm a morning guy—the earlier I can get something started, the better. When I first began hiring employees for my company, I held an unconscious expectation that they would all be morning people, too. I had to figure out in a hurry that coming at good, talented, smart people who just happen to despise everything that happens before 9 AM with my sky-high morning energy might be a recipe for discontent and inefficiency—the total opposite of the culture I wanted to create.

I have long believed that one of the laziest, most detrimental statements a leader can make is: *I should have known*. But there I was. Once this idea had my attention, it was obvious. But it would have been all too easy for me to realize that after it was too late.

As we structure our days and our stories, it's difficult to stay disciplined toward a clearly determined objective. But it is *impossible* to be disciplined toward a fuzzy one. No expectations? No corresponding self-view?

No progress.

If you want to structure a life that leads you toward success, you've got to set expectations.

Believe me, when I finally got out of bed after my first marathon, I didn't miraculously change my habits. The voice in my head that whispers *just ten more minutes* when the alarm goes off didn't go away. My will was not ironclad. Many mornings, I wanted to stay under the covers, and many evenings the big recliner in the basement was calling my name.

But my expectations for myself were clear and getting clearer: *Be* a runner. *Set* a habit. *Do* the work. And every single time I made a choice that was consistent with my self-view, those expectations got a little more real, and the structures I'd created got a little more solid.

The truth is, our decisions weigh heavily in favor of who we *believe* we are; and when we follow through, even just a day, then two, then three—a natural momentum takes hold. And one day you realize that rather than wrestling with the version of you that wants to stay in bed, your feet are already on the floor. You didn't even have to think about it.

That was the day I went trotting down the pavement with my head high, thinking, *Oh yeah. This is who I AM.*

> **The truth is, our decisions weigh heavily in favor of who we believe we are; and when we follow through, even just a day, then two, then three—a natural momentum takes hold. And one day you realize that rather than wrestling with the version of you that wants to stay in bed, your feet are already on the floor. You didn't even have to think about it.**

STRUCTURING PRINCIPLE #4: GET REAL ABOUT TIME

If you really want to get a handle on how the structure of your days is shaping your story, zero in on one day and put its structure under a microscope.

> ❯ When and how did you sleep?
> ❯ What time did you wake?
> ❯ What did you do with the fourteen or sixteen or eighteen hours you were active? Each of them.
> ❯ How many of those hours were spent doing something congruent with your values and goals? Be easy on yourself in your assessments, because this isn't a gotcha exercise. Just ask: *Which hours were worth my while?*
> ❯ If you had that day to do over, what would you do differently?

However you answer that last question, do *that* tomorrow.

I know; it's tougher than it sounds. But the truth is, most people underestimate what they can accomplish in small increments of time—ten minutes, an hour, one day—and they overestimate what they can do in a month or a year or a lifetime. How many times in your life have you thought or said *I don't have enough time for that today* when you're facing an immediate demand? Every month? Every week? Every day?

But what about the flip side? *I'll have plenty of time for that later.*

Really?

Sometimes we meet people who are wising up to this, who will look us in the eye and say, "I'm not sure how much time I have. Let's do it now." But they are exceedingly rare. Some have walked through tragedy and come away enlightened. Some, like Bronnie Ware's patients, are coming to the end of their lives. And some, like Ware herself, have become wise through observation. If you're like me, you hear each of them with a corresponding thud in your gut—because you recognize the fundamental and universal truth in their urgency.

As someone who helps people identify their goals, work toward them, and better themselves and their situations, I've learned not just through my own experience but through those of thousands of clients that no one should ever underestimate the power of thirty minutes a day. It can make the difference, for example, between getting fit or staying sedentary. Thirty minutes a day times seven days is 3.5 hours a week. Fourteen hours a month. If you spent 160 hours this year walking on a treadmill, wouldn't you be healthier? That same thirty minutes can be deployed to any purpose that matters to you: Read about a new subject. Learn a language. Take up a hobby that brings you joy.

Which brings us to the catch—a big one. The only way you're going to be able to structure your life to support that thirty minutes (or hour, or more) is if you schedule it on time that you own.

If you schedule your "me time" in a part of your day you've committed to someone else, you're creating a structure that's going to fall apart. Example: For all the years I was a dad with my daughters at home, I could reasonably expect that "my" time ended when my girls got out of bed. From then on it was family time, work time, then family time again. Most weekdays, that took me from 6 or 7 AM until 8 or 9 at night. There's no question that when you're raising a family and holding down a job, the parameters of me time can be a little tight.

But there is always a margin—a place where you can stake even a small claim on time for yourself. Maybe right now you can only spare thirty minutes. If so, start there. Personally, I started out claiming a little time during the earliest hours of the day—and it was such a game changer in my life that I was eventually able to find a big block of time there—from 4 to 6 AM. See-the-sunrise hours. Once I got accustomed to getting out of bed and prowling the house while everybody else slept, I found those hours to be just about magical. In recent years, this window of time has become so valuable and rewarding to me that I've made it a goal to see the sunrise each morning, 365 days of the year.

When I'm home, I see it from the deck behind my house, where the view is spectacular, and I can feel grateful for whatever I've accomplished so far for the day. But some of the most amazing sunrises I see happen when I'm traveling. On business trips, I make a point to time my run around the sunrise. Sometimes I choose a noteworthy destination to enhance the experience. Running around state capitol buildings, for example, is one of my favorite sunrise experiences. At this writing, I've run around eighteen of them—some of those many times (shout out to Des Moines and its capitol's golden dome). I can't wait to add to this list.

In truth, those early-morning hours are the key to creating momentum for my entire day.

And they're true "me time." My family is incredibly supportive, even when I want to do something on their time—but in those two hours each morning, I know I am only accountable to myself. I read. I run. I go to the gym. And it's no exaggeration to say that by the time my workday starts, I've already got a big win. I've got momentum like nobody's business.

Is 4 AM a solution for everybody? Probably not. But there is a structure that works for you. The secret for most people who keep traditional business hours is to look to the bookends of the day: mornings and evenings. Call dibs on bigger blocks of time during your weekends or other days off. Put yourself on your calendar—in ink. So many people are convinced that they don't own *any* of their time, but that's not true. Some things are less flexible than others, but there's always a way to take back thirty minutes or an hour. Start there. Compromise a little sleep. Compromise an hour of TV one or two nights a week. Enlist the assistance of your family (or hired help) for a time-consuming chore and give yourself that time. Only you can decide what is enough and what is too much for you, but when you want to commit to betterment, commit to owning that time.

How many times in your life have you thought or said I don't have enough time for that today *when you're facing an immediate demand?*

Every month? Every week? Every day?

But what about the flip side? I'll have plenty of time for that later.

Really?

STRUCTURING PRINCIPLE #5: EMBRACE PROCESS OVER OUTCOME

The GOAT of marathon running is a man named Eliud Kipchoge, and at this writing he is a two-time Olympic champion and the owner of four of the six fastest marathon times on record. In 2018, Kipchoge finished the Berlin race with a then record time of two hours, one minute, and thirty-nine seconds. (He would later break this record himself, but that's a story for another day.)

The next year, in 2019, Kipchoge threw himself into the pursuit of a very specific and lofty goal: running a sub-two-hour marathon.

Shaving less than two minutes off a personal record for such a long race might sound feasible on first consideration, but the truth is it had never in the history of the world been done. Many experts in the field flatly denied it was possible. A sub-two-hour marathon was like a 110-mile-per-hour pitch in baseball or a quintuple axel in figure skating—a feat seemingly beyond the reach of human capability.

Kipchoge went to work anyway, running 120 to 140 miles each week—laser focused on adjusting his best time by that all-important minute as he pounded out each step. His sponsors and team scouted which city, route, pavement, time of year, hydration delivery system, shoes, and even what arrangement of runners around him would offer the most favorable conditions.

And then, on October 12, 2019, Eliud Kipchoge launched his attempt in Vienna.

One hour, fifty-nine minutes, and forty seconds later it was over, and the 26.2 mile run-time record was shattered.

The BBC called Kipchoge's feat "a moon-landing moment." The *Wall Street Journal*'s headline declared, "Kipchoge Smashes Running's Last Great Barrier."

But *The Atlantic*'s headline struck a wildly different tone, proclaiming the run "The Greatest, Fakest World Record."

And so went reactions around the globe. Half the world stood in awe, shouting, *This is unbelievable!* The other half protested, saying, *This doesn't count*—discrediting the thousands of miles Kipchoge ran, and every time he put one foot in front of the other to cover them. The critics seemed convinced that optimizing conditions somehow lessened this monumental accomplishment.

As I watched this event and its coverage unfold from half the world away, there was a critical lesson in it for me—one I believe every person who works to structure a life of substance and fulfillment would do well to take to heart:

Do. Your. Process. Run your steps. Give your time and energy in the best way you know how. Sometimes the wind will be at your back and sometimes it will be in your face. Sometimes you will succeed and sometimes you will come up short. Sometimes you'll get credit and sometimes your efforts will be unsung. And there will *always* be someone in your orbit who will attribute whatever you've done—win or lose—to circumstances that were beyond your control.

The fact is, if you want to have success, you have to get rid of your circumstance bias and focus on what *you can do.* In the history of the world, nobody ever won a footrace they didn't run. In the history of the world, "market conditions" never bought or sold a product. In the history of the world, no parent ever taught their kid to tie a shoe or ride a bike or bake a cake without showing up and moving from step to step.

By all means, control what you can. Take an edge where you can find one. But after that, there's nothing left to do but the work.

QUESTIONS
TO CONSIDER

> Who do you want to be next? A world-class parent? A rock-star spouse? A business tycoon? An athlete? An artist? You don't have to choose one thing—in fact, you shouldn't—but it's nearly impossible to have true time management unless you know what you're striving to become. Consider one facet of your story to work on right now.

> What structures, schedules, and habits underpin your days? Are you the architect of those routines? Or does it feel like *they're* driving *you?*

> When was the last time you deliberately shook up the structures in your life? Would you benefit from the new

perspective a reset would provide? What could you do tomorrow to make it all feel a little bit new?

> What habits and routines do you have on automatic? Are those helping you feel accomplished and fulfilled? Are any of them getting in your way? Habits have power—for good or for trouble—but the only way to assess them is with deliberate scrutiny. Take a wider view and ask: *What is the habit here? Why do it this way? Is it serving me at my very highest level?* If you're not sure where to start, choose one slice of your day to examine.

> What habit do you *wish* you had? What would it take to start building it today? Can you give it ten minutes on your calendar each day for a week as a trial run? Research tells us that it takes somewhere between twenty-one and fifty-nine days for a repeated behavior to become automatic—for the unconscious part of your brain to start taking it over. What habit do you love the idea of enough to honor a small commitment for that long?

> Where's the "me time" in your planner? It shouldn't take a magnifying glass to find it! Consider building more of it in the "bookends" of the day—early morning and late evening—on time no one else owns.

> Do a twenty-four-hour test and consider: How many of your waking hours were spent in activities actually congruent with your values and goals? If you had that day to do over, what would you do differently? Pick one small action and make an adjustment. Exercising that margin of control may just create the momentum you need to create lasting change.

▪ CANNONBALL BOOK CLUB FAVORITES ▪

The Molecule of More: How a Single Chemical in Your Brain Drives Love, Sex, and Creativity—and Will Determine the Fate of the Human Race

Daniel Z. Lieberman and Michael Long

CHAD'S NOTE: This is easily one of the best science-based books I've ever read. Lieberman does such an amazing job of explaining the concept of dopamine as a behavior driver that I found the book immediately applicable to my daily life. This title is an invaluable tool in recognizing patterns that disrupt your routines and your best intentions. It's rare for a book to have a lasting impact on behavior, but *The Molecule of More* teaches you how to work *with* your dopamine system instead of living life at the mercy of it. It's tremendously eye-opening.

> *If you live under a bridge, dopamine makes you want a tent.*
> *If you live in a tent, dopamine makes you want a house . . .*
> *The dopamine circuits in the brain can be stimulated only by the possibility of whatever is shiny and new, never mind how perfect things are at the moment. The dopamine motto is "More."*

The Upside of Stress: Why Stress Is Good for You, and How to Get Good at It

Kelly McGonigal, PhD

CHAD'S NOTE: Most people look at stress as something that will tear you apart, but this book goes deeper. It explains that sweet spot in which stress becomes a motivator, a path to growth, and a portal to new understanding. McGonigal's book will make you more likely to invite good stress into your life, and more capable of recognizing and avoiding destructive stress.

Everyone has an Everest. Whether it's a climb you chose, or a circumstance you find yourself in, you're in the middle of an important journey. Can you imagine a climber scaling the wall of ice at Everest's Lhotse Face and saying, "This is such a hassle"? Or spending the first night in the mountain's "death zone" and thinking, "I don't need this stress"?

The climber knows the context of his stress. It has personal meaning to him; he has chosen it.

8

CHOOSE YOUR CIRCLES

Cast every role with care.

Who's the hero of your story? Who's in your supporting cast?

The heart of every good story lies with its characters. Our life stories are no different. They're shaped by the kind of characters we become and who we cast in the circles around us.

Cast in this case is a verb—an action you take (or don't take). It's looking for and choosing the right person for the right role. Or taking a step back, looking at someone who's already there, and asking tough questions about whether that relationship is helping or hurting your health, happiness, and growth.

For a long time I didn't bother with any of that. I didn't even think about it. The universe sent people into my life; they slid into their roles by intention or by default, and I was oblivious to how much their presence mattered. On the rare occasions I did make choices—scrutinizing who I was hanging out with or allowing to get close—my preferences were skewed to people who made it easy for me to remain stuck in my rut. I gravitated to friends and coworkers who were quick to commiserate with my complaints, content to ignore my failures, and more interested in gratification than in growth.

In those years, those decades, I was not the author of my life in any meaningful way. In fact, I may have been the living, breathing incarnation of entrepreneur and author Jim Rohn's famous observation that "you are the average of the five people you spend the most time with."

Hang around with five friends who hate their jobs and you'll likely learn to dislike yours. Hang around with five hard-partying pals and you might wind up with a drinking problem (or a late-for-work problem). Hang around with five people who treat others with disrespect and you may soak up some of that negative energy and make it part of your own personality.

Luckily, there are more hopeful possibilities: Hang around with five athletes and you may decide it's time to get fit. Hang around with five principled leaders and you could deepen your strength and influence. Hang around with five friends who strive to be generous and impactful—and some of that commitment to betterment might rub off on you.

Rohm's adage references five people, but our circles tend to be bigger than that, and even if our behaviors don't become precisely the *average* of those around us, we're undoubtedly influenced by them. Researchers in group dynamics have looked at this time and again, trying to understand who impacts our behaviors and attitudes and how it happens.

One study, for example, looked at the fitness of freshman US Air Force Academy cadets. Since cadets are randomly assigned to squadrons that then eat, sleep, study, and train together, they make fantastic subjects for researchers studying social influence. In this case, they monitored individual cadets and squadron groups for fitness metrics. Reading about the study, I guessed at the results—and figured fitness is an individual thing. The cadets were all young, healthy, and following similar workout regimens, so of course their range would be narrower than that of a bunch of strangers off the street. Beyond that baseline, though, I thought each squadron would have high achievers, moderate achievers, and low achievers.

I was wrong. At the end of the study, results did show a range of fitness levels across all participants—but there was almost no differentiation *within* squadrons. If cadets A, B, and C were all part of a single squadron, spending most of their time together, their metrics were a near match for one another, but not for members of other squadrons. The kicker? The data suggested that each squadron gravitated toward the health level of its least fit, least motivated member.

When it was published in the *Journal of Public Economics* in August 2011, this study was titled "Is Poor Fitness Contagious?" The evidence suggested that it is.

It makes you wonder what other traits, habits, and attitudes might be catching, doesn't it?

The people you surround yourself with can lift you up, drag you down, and influence your personality. This doesn't just apply to those of us who are easily influenced. It happens to leaders and followers, to the charismatic and the dull, to entrepreneurs and employees.

In my coaching practice, I see this concept in action every day, but in the best possible way. I watch members of my leadership groups gradually elevate one another's attitudes and ideas over the course of a year as we work together both remotely and in person. These are some of the most highly motivated executives I've encountered, and it shows in how they connect. On a recent call, one of these participants summed up by telling the group, "I feel like my closest friends are on this call. You support and challenge me. I'm really not finding that anywhere else in my life."

On another call, a coaching client in his late sixties spoke up. This is a man whose entire life has steered him away from self-reflection. He grew up with a my-way-or-the-highway father; he spent years in the military; he forged an exceptional career in a male-dominated, highly competitive nuts-and-bolts industry. This is someone who'd be the first to tell you that until he began working with a coach, he'd rarely experienced an introspective moment in his life. There simply wasn't room for it.

He was tied to a lifestyle and a leadership style, and he'd been holding on for so long that he'd lost sight of the fact that he could choose change.

When someone this intelligent, accomplished, and driven chooses to SHIFT, think bigger, and apply himself to becoming a better man, well, *look out*. There's no ceiling on that betterment potential. This is someone who opened himself up to listening and learning again after decades of operating by force of habit—and a lot of the credit for that goes to his leadership group peers.

What's happened since? He's reopened lines of communication with an adult child who'd drifted away. He's hired a trainer and committed to working out twice a week. He held a summit with key employees to ask questions and listen to answers—an event that led to revising a number of outdated and micromanaging policies. With a new level of trust in place, he's motivated his team like never before—and increased sales numbers reflect their enthusiasm.

Time and again, he's brought all those changes and his growth right back to our leadership group, where he pours encouragement and validation into other members.

I sign off from those meetings feeling like the luckiest guy in the world. I get to work with these extraordinary people, get to encourage and witness their growth, and get to see how their group dynamic translates to greater life satisfaction, happier employees, and stronger businesses.

Each gathering of these voices serves to remind us that casting the roles, big and small, in our lives is critical work. It's work that's often overlooked—at our peril.

CONCENTRIC CIRCLES

The question of finding your people, of course, is *how*. How do we choose our circles? How do we ensure we have the support we need? How do we push toxic characters to the fringes, and how do we bring people we respect and value closer? And how do we do it all without putting up walls against new voices and personalities?

For me, the answer lies in imagining the people we cast in our lives in concentric circles. Consider them your own personal solar system:

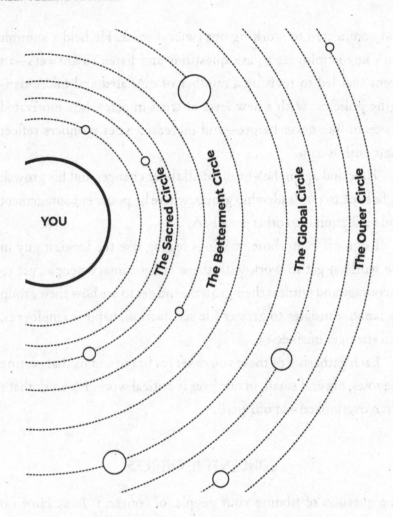

> **The Center:** You are in the middle. It's your universe.
> **The Sacred Circle:** Your ride-or-die, 'til-death-do-us-part, most-treasured family and friends.
> **The Betterment Circle:** People who make you better, who are each in their own way supporting your growth, success, and happiness (and you theirs).
> **The Global Circle:** Colleagues, peers, friends, relatives, neighbors, waiters, the mail carrier, and even strangers

who are in your orbit. People who have your goodwill, but not necessarily your attention.

> **The *Outer Circle:*** Voices you choose to keep at a distance or actively repel.

In order to keep your life open to new ideas and energy (and in order to have an escape hatch for energy vampires and unhealthy influences), the rings are fluid. People move between them all the time. Choosing your circles isn't a one-time event; it's something you'll be doing as long as you're alive.

Let's look at each circle:

You at the Center

Most of us have been conditioned our whole lives to keep our self-image small, to keep our contributions proportionate, to shun the spotlight. As a coach—both in the business world and in kids' sports—I encourage my team members to go another way. I want them to grow, stretch, and be proud and confident. Each of us is the sun in our own solar system. I am emphatic about acknowledgment of this—a passion that started courtside in a gym, with a bunch of basketball players who just could not sink their foul shots.

I coached my daughters' basketball teams for more than a decade and loved it. Then one season, the girls suddenly and inexplicably stopped being able to make free throws. Over the span of a few games, their stats plummeted, creating a crisis. They were sinking less than half—a dreadful stat for a skill that even a young team should be able to master.

As this low success rate continued, game after game and week after week, I could see the toll it was taking on my players. When they stepped up to the line, their faces were etched with worry, their eyes were panicked, and their bodies were tense. It was all too easy to see what they were thinking as each in turn came to the foul line. It was a litany of *don'ts: Don't miss. Don't blow it while everyone is watching. Don't ruin this for the team.*

Each week, the team became a little more desperate and negative. They were routinely (if inadvertently) telling themselves they were incapable of success, and that mentality was practically assuring their failure.

With the situation getting out of hand, I knew we had to do something to restore confidence, to help each team member back into a mindset of capability. Each needed a reminder that she was an athlete worthy of respect and success. Everybody takes foul shots. Everybody needs to be confident in them.

At practice, I asked everyone on the team to raise a hand and point one finger in the air. I said, "Here's the situation: Fourth quarter and we're down by one. There's no time left on the clock. Your opponent gets a technical and someone has to go to the line. On the count of three, I want you to point to the girl who's going to take those shots for us.

"Ready?" I asked, looking around this small circle of frustrated young athletes.

"One. Two. Three. Point!"

All but one of the girls pointed to somebody else.

I asked the one who'd pointed to herself why she'd done it.

She answered, with full confidence, "I'll make the shot."

Boom!

That simple, logical response sent a ripple through the team. Other girls were quick to say they'd *wanted* to point to themselves. But, well, that had felt like showing too much ego.

Here's the thing about ego. I believe it stands for *Edging God Out*—taking credit for greatness that isn't yours alone. But that doesn't mean we are anything less than great. In fact, the opposite is true. Those girls needed to step into the confidence of knowing they were *born* great.

Their job was to hone their skills, believe in themselves and each other, and let that greatness shine. Each deserved star-athlete confidence. Each deserved to be able to look to herself when a critical moment came along.

So we practiced. We did power poses. We told stories around their efforts. And they gained a little confidence. Before the next game, I told my team, "From now on, when you step to the foul line, I want you to look over at me on the bench, I want you to point to yourself, and I want you to say, '*I've got this.*'"

The next season, and for the five years the team continued to play together, those girls shot 85 percent or better from the line. No one player can carry a team to that stat. Each of them realized she could rise to a challenge and excel, even under pressure.

What they had, what they cultivated, was star-of-the-story energy.

How about you? Do you point to yourself? Do you acknowledge that your needs and growth, your contributions and connections are your priority? When you claim your place at the center of your small universe, are you deliberate about it? Taking control, accomplishing more, feeling better, nurturing relationships, and doing great things—they all start with putting yourself center stage in your own life.

The trouble is, a lot of us have a hard time with that, because self-prioritizing feels, well, selfish.

The Selfishness Paradox

As I write this, I've seen references to everything from plain old narcissism to something called "toxic main character syndrome" in recent days. And I realize we can't have a conversation about each of us being the center of our own universe without considering the necessary selfishness of that concept.

The truth is, the idea of betterment usually *does* start selfishly. It starts at a moment when you feel utterly compelled to change yourself. There are only a couple circumstances that can get you to that point: desperation or inspiration. In either, sooner or later you realize that in order to accomplish any meaningful SHIFT, you've got to turn your focus inward. You ask questions, revisit stories, reconsider behaviors, and recalibrate your self-view—all on your way to rewriting your story to fit the life you want.

So yeah, the roots of betterment are selfish. But this is selfishness for the greater good.

I've yet to meet anyone in my decade of training and coaching who undergoes a journey of transformation and somehow turns *into* a selfish jerk. Instead, once they center themselves, take care of themselves, and begin to make progress, they have *more* strength, energy, joy, and dedication to bring when they show up for others.

My own journey to making peace with necessary selfishness started when I met my wife. To paraphrase *When Harry Met*

Sally, I wanted what she was having. She was confident, smart, and unapologetic in her pursuit of her education, her career, and her happiness. Her energy was vibrant and undeniable, and it was catching. It made me look at what I was doing and where I was going, and it made me feel desperate to get better.

I didn't change overnight. I didn't take a straight path. I quit a job when I didn't have another one. I took wrong turns and ran into dead ends. At times, I wallowed in my fears and insecurities. In all honesty, if I hadn't been able to turn my energy inward during that time—to selfishly work on *me* through a long phase of change—I might have ended up right back where I started: Killing time in an unfulfilling job. Wracked with self-doubt. Seeing myself as a victim, a villain, or a sidekick.

Instead, I stuck it out long enough to see small changes, and then bigger ones. And eventually I turned a corner I hadn't even known existed—to realizing that my betterment, my determination, and my energy could be contagious, too.

By some miracle, when I started sharing my story, I found I was capable of *contributing* to another person's growth, and then another, and another.

> *I've yet to meet anyone in my decade of training and coaching who undergoes a journey of transformation and somehow turns into a selfish jerk. Instead, once they center themselves, they have more strength, energy, joy, and dedication to bring when they show up for others.*

The secret, I think, is this: When you commit to betterment, you don't just change your own life. You change critical facets of your relationships. You may even create change that echoes through organizations and generations. A few examples:

> My daughters were unquestionably raised by a better father than they would have had if I hadn't started down my "selfish" path to betterment. My commitment to raising them as strong, powerful women deepened alongside my own growth.

> An executive client who struggled with feeling unworthy of her position used her "selfish" pursuit of betterment to finally become confident and comfortable in her seat at the table. Once she did, she revolutionized the culture of her department, instituting changes that led to a more loyal, more productive team.

> A coaching client whose "selfish" journey toward personal growth led him to vow he'd tell his son *I love you* every day. You can't tell me that growing up in a home where you hear *I love you* all the time versus one where those words go unsaid doesn't influence your trajectory. It may even change the way that boy raises his own kids one day.

Almost every story I've shared of a client's personal growth in this book has had a positive impact beyond the individual who decided to claim the role of star of their story. Each has created a chain of betterment that continues to grow.

Perhaps the most overlooked part of centering yourself, of choosing to be the lead actor in the story of your life, is that once you're secure in your own position, you're a thousand times better equipped to show up for everyone else.

We see this most of all in great leaders, in people who live centered, strong, and ready to contribute to others. There's this whole debate in leadership literature about what role they should take. Do great leaders get out in front of each charge? Do they coach from the sidelines? Do they eat first? Or last? Do they hold themselves apart? Do they confess their vulnerability?

The answer? *All of it.* Truly great leaders are secure enough to meet the needs that are in front of them. They know there is a time to teach and a time to learn. A time to get out in front and a time to let someone else step forward. A time to be patient and a time to go turbo. They're able to assess each circumstance, adapt, and deliver.

Once you're confident as the star of your personal universe, you won't have any problem choosing to step in and out of the roles that allow you to lead.

Sacred Circle

What if you decided, regardless of your career, *This month I'm going to make as much money and have as much impact as I can—in the minimum of time I can manage—and then I'm* going home *to enjoy the people and activities I've been busting my ass for.*

What if you announced it at your office today?

When I pose this scenario during a leadership training session or a company's keynote, the audience gets *very* quiet. People look at their feet. Some steal furtive glances at their managers and CEOs. It almost feels as if I've spilled a dirty secret—as if we didn't all already know that we work for two reasons: to make money and to have an impact.

Some of us are focused on profits and paychecks. Some derive our greatest satisfaction from making a difference for our employees, clients, customers, students, or even strangers who benefit from what we create or do. Most of us are somewhere in the middle. We want to contribute; we want to profit. And at the end of the day, we want to take all of that home to the people in our *sacred circle*.

Who are they? That's easy: They're the family members and treasured friends for whom you'd walk over hot coals or eat dirt. They're spouses and partners, kids, parents, and siblings. They're the friends with whom you never have to pretend—because they know you almost as well as you know yourself. They're the people with whom you break bread; the ones you stand up for at weddings, baptisms, and funerals; the ones whose needs and wants you keep at top of mind; the people you are sworn to love and protect.

You may have just two people in this small circle, or four, or ten. You'd do just about anything for them, right?

And yet you probably don't. We all fail at this sometimes. We take the people in this circle for granted. We put them off for more pressing "priorities." We tune them out because we're so sure we already know what they're going to say.

How does that happen?

I can tell you that after asking this question of nearly ten thousand people, the answer almost always comes down to work.

Of course your work is important. That's key to so many measurable and unmeasurable metrics of success and fulfillment. But being committed to something and being handcuffed to it are two entirely different things. Don't get handcuffed to your career and lose sight of the reason you do everything you do.

Go home. Make time. Listen. Ask questions.

Through my podcast I've met some amazing and accomplished entrepreneurs, authors, innovators, and other impactful people who are changing the world. And I can tell you that after years of doing this, after more than a hundred episodes, the ones who most impress and inspire me are the individuals who never, not for a minute, lose sight of the fact that there is no substitute for giving the people in your sacred circle the time and attention they deserve. I've met billionaires who change diapers. Owners of hundred-million-dollar companies who coach their kids' sports. CEOs of huge, highly profitable companies who put their phones in a drawer when they get home at night and give their partners their undivided attention.

Not everyone in the world is lucky enough to have people in this circle. If you are blessed with them, be present for them. They are a source of energy, strength, faith, and fun, and that has to flow both ways. You pour into your tribe, and they pour into you.

Extras, Anyone?

Around now, your thoughts may turn to somebody in your life who's *technically* in this circle—but boy, would you like to shake them loose.

It was Bishop Desmond Tutu who said, "You don't choose your family. They are God's gift to you." I believe this to my core. But I'm not naïve. I realize that sometimes life puts people close to us—even in our families—who can't be counted on to honor the trust of the sacred circle. It's in these instances that your freedom to choose who you cast in your circles gives you the agency to make a change. Because while the first part of *casting* characters is about finding your people, the second is about figuring out what roles you're going to assign them. We choose both the person and the role.

You've seen the credits after a movie, right? You've got stars and costars. You've got a supporting cast. And you've got bit parts and extras—most of whom don't even get a name.

So let's say you've had the questionable fortune of being given, by birth or by marriage, someone in your life with a personality you just pray is *not* contagious. You try to keep your distance. In some cases, you may not be able to (or even want to) cut that person out of your life, but you can surely rethink the role in which you see them. The angry, racist, rude in-law? It's within your power to demote them from *trusted elder* to *distant relative*. That's a great role, one in which that person is mostly seen and not heard.

You can choose to do this, too, with characters who haunt your life. I know this one well. Choosing to cast the father who left my family as a near stranger who missed out on the joys of our family serves me infinitely better than holding him in my mind as the ghost of a life that might have been. In making that change, I gave myself a whole new peace.

Betterment Circle

At Cannonball Moments, one of our flagship programs is a year-long engagement called the *Betterment Circle*. It's a support system that's open to clients who have a deep commitment to personal and professional growth. It unites those clients with each other, with me, with Cannonball's amazing trainers, and with experts in fields ranging from economics to psychology, neuroscience to fitness, and, of course, leadership.

The purpose of this group is to foster a community in which every single person feels emboldened to pursue betterment. I don't care if you want to be a world-class athlete, a game-changing innovator, an inspiring leader, a devoted and equal partner—or all of those things. Whatever betterment looks like to you, that's what the group is there to help you pursue.

Participants have called this group "nothing less than life-changing"—and that's exactly what it is for me, year after year.

Here's the thing: Each of us needs a personal betterment circle. Outside of your sacred circle, this group is the one with the most potential to profoundly impact your life. It's comprised of people who facilitate and root for your growth and success. And unlike your sacred circle, which is likely populated both by family members you choose and those you simply choose to embrace, the betterment circle should be full of people you've considered on their merits and *invited* in.

Who makes the cut?

Start with friends, colleagues, and mentors who offer you complete and compassionate candor. They're people who see you, warts and all, and who care about you always. But they don't do pity parties, and they are unrepentant in calling you on your shit.

Let me tell you, the first time I found myself with a friend who said, "You're better than that," I was floored. What kind of friendship was *that*? Aren't friends the people who tell you you're right? Who say your efforts—even when they're meager—are enough? Who buy you a beer and say, "Man, that whole thing was rigged anyway"?

You can choose to have those kinds of friends, sure, but they don't belong in your betterment circle. The people in this circle are the ones with whom you can lay down your ego, get real about the kind of person you want to be, and expect them to say, "I want that for you. How can you start?"

When you do get started, the people in this circle will abide your efforts. They won't judge. They won't try to hold you back. When you surround yourself with people who make it okay to try, to experiment (even when those experiments end in failure), and to evolve, you're on your way to growth.

Betterment-level mentorship, friendship, and partnership is rare, and it's priceless. As you build this circle, remember that it turns on reciprocity. Share what you can. Help whenever possible. Offer support and show gratitude always.

Who Is Leading You?

I'm not sure any great betterment circle was ever made up of just friends. In order to truly grow, we need leaders just as much as comrades.

When I was twenty-one, working on the very bottom rung of the hotel service ladder, I had a manager who did his damnedest to be a leader for me. He praised my successes. He coached me through my failures. He was forgiving (but never approving) when I was late. He expected me to work hard. He'd ask me what I was reading, what more I wanted in my life, how I saw my career shaping up.

I was oblivious to the fact that this was someone who was trying to help me. Someone who believed in my potential and wanted to see me better myself. I thought the guy was just a pain in the ass.

I think about him often now, because even though I wasn't ready back then—and he probably figured he was wasting his breath—that man's efforts make me a better leader these days. I am more patient, more empathetic, and more persistent because of him. I have more faith in people who are coming up short because of him. I know that even when I am tapped to lead someone who frustrates me, I owe them the same depth of goodwill and optimism that manager offered me.

He was in my betterment circle before I was even capable of believing that such a thing existed.

To be clear, when I talk about leaders, I'm always mindful that leadership does not come part and parcel with the title on anybody's door. It's not inherent in any position. I've met many people who, on paper, *should* be world-class leaders—but who are not. Sometimes they're the richest. Sometimes the smartest. Sometimes the most powerful. But leadership isn't defined by wealth, intellect, or power. It's defined by the way you foster excellence and growth in other people. When you become the person who connects, who asks questions, who helps another person step into their own talents, skills, power, and happiness—*that's* when you are a leader.

When you look for leadership in this critical circle, you'll recognize it in the people you want to emulate and learn from. They're the ones who are ahead of you on some path (though not necessarily on every path), leaving tracks. They're the ones who handle ethical and moral challenges with grace. They're the ones who've honed their negotiation and conflict resolution skills to an art. They're the ones who seem to have all that energy you're working to find in yourself.

Leaders come from all walks of life—not just from the C-suite of your company, the rectory of your church, or the halls of academia. Pay more attention to the way people make you feel—make you want to be better and do more—than you do to their business cards, and you'll find the right ones for you.

Your Experts

By now you know that I don't want anyone reading these pages to settle for being great in just one area of their life. I want you to have success across the board, and I believe you can do it. One of the most overlooked ways to make this happen is by—wait for it—*asking for help.*

It's not a radical idea, but it sure can be a difficult one to put into practice. We don't want to ask for favors. We don't want to demand more notice than we deserve. We don't want to come off as needy or uninformed or too ambitious for our own good.

Rest assured that anyone who makes their way into your betterment circle is not going to judge you on those criteria. They're going to want to help. The key here is in understanding your own needs and seeking out the guides you need. I have the closest thing to a personal board of directors in my circle—people who help me in my personal growth, my career, my loving relationships, my faith, my health, my finances, and my cannonball moments. I am always interviewing for seats on this board (whether or not the interviewee is aware of it!). And I realize I'm always being measured on my ability to fill those needs for others.

A betterment circle is small. Not everyone you consult with is going to be in it. But if you frequently and thoughtfully take stock of your own areas of priority, considering where you most need guidance, then you'll walk through your life with your eyes wide open to finding the right people to cast.

It's like playing the game banana, but with potentially life-enriching guidance as the prize for winning instead of just bragging rights for spotting all those yellow cars.

Global Circle

The biggest social group, by far, is the global circle. I'm not talking about everyone in the whole wide world, but rather the people who know your name or your face or your reputation. This group is a kind of casting waiting room. Some of its characters may eventually make their way into closer circles; others may end up moving to the outermost ring.

This is a circle where you may want to be known, where you can build brand awareness and personal credibility. And it's a circle where people can move closer, maybe reaching the point where you stop and have a conversation, or even where you break bread together. This circle is a vast pool of potential contacts, colleagues, friends, trusted advisors, and even members of your sacred circle.

My advice on dealing with everyone in this circle is this: Be curious and be kind. Each of us in it shares the same basic human need to be seen, heard, and acknowledged. And the thing is, you never know who from this group may one day be sitting in that closest circle, with the two of you taking care of each other.

Some of the most momentous decisions we make in our lives originate in how we interact with people in our global circles. I know this from personal experience. In fact, when I first met my wife, I almost missed my chance. We had a crappy first date. I was a jerk. Months later, when I ran into her again, she called me on it, and I was shocked.

And then I took a deep breath—and asked her to go out with me again.

I don't know why she agreed. It wasn't because I deserved it. I think it's probably because she was curious and kind. I think she wanted to know if there was more to me.

What happened after that—the love story of a marriage and a family and laughter and joy—could have gone another way. We could have discovered, halfway through that second date, that we didn't have much to talk about, or that one of us didn't have a sense of humor, or that our values were so completely unaligned that a relationship could never work.

It happens. People's values aren't out in front of them like billboards. You can't read them from a distance. You have to get close to figure it out. You have to pay attention to the snapshots that make up their big picture. But if you don't come in curious, if you don't start from kindness, you'll never find out. And you could easily miss something worthwhile.

Much as I love talking about the story that put me on the path to the life I have today—the one where I get the girl and get to build an amazing life—it's important to acknowledge that no matter how curious and kind you are, you'll still meet people you must push to the outer edges of this circle. Sometimes these are the people you'd least expect.

This happened to me when I worked with a prominent author and influencer—someone whose work has been an inspiration to me. I couldn't wait to meet him, couldn't believe my luck in being able to be in the same room. I didn't go in curious; I went in eager and idolizing.

It took almost no time to realize that was all a mistake. Persona isn't personality. The flesh-and-blood version of this person was dismissive, disconnected, and unable to find it in his heart to say *hello*, or *please* or *thank you* to strangers—something we learn to do in kindergarten. His interactions with the people in his global circle were a lesson in what not to do.

There was nothing to do but move him to the outer edge—and then move on with curiosity and kindness to someone else.

The Outer Circle

Every time I hear a Billy Joel song, I sing along. I know every word and melody. I'm not a singer or a musician. I've never spent a single minute applying myself to learning those lyrics. They just seeped in like water, going all the way to my roots.

When I hear those songs now, my thoughts inevitably follow two separate tracks. The first calls up one of the truly joyful moments from my childhood—the night my entire family went to a Billy Joel concert. I have no idea how we afforded those tickets (even for seats that were practically in the rafters), but that didn't matter to me. I was thirteen years old, at my first concert, surrounded by my tribe. I could feel the energy and the music thrumming through that arena and straight into me. I jumped and danced and sang at the top of my lungs. The scene is still vivid in my memories (and it made me a lifelong fan).

The second train of thought is one I didn't wake up to until much later in life, but it's something I think about a lot now: The reason I know all the words to those songs is because we learn more *unconsciously*, where some 95 percent of our brain activity takes place, than we do *consciously*. Words, images, and concepts do, in fact, seep in.

It's no big deal when I'm wandering around the house singing "Piano Man" or "Scenes from an Italian Restaurant" (and yeah, I know I'm showing my age here)—those songs lift me up. They make me happy. They boost my energy and inspire me to get creative.

But what if the influences that are seeping in are more subversive—and what if they're far enough out toward the periphery of my life that I'm not always noticing they're around?

They're seeping in all the same. This is, potentially, an entire circle of forces that endlessly stoke me to feel fear, worry, disgust, and complacency.

What are these forces? There's no single culprit; but twenty-four-hour news, toxic social media feeds, and a bottomless pit of streaming programming are just a few of the players that come to mind. Sometimes it seems like they're out to drown us in negativity. And they're not going anywhere—because there is profit in them. You've heard the long-held adage in journalism that "if it bleeds, it leads." Stories about violence, scandal, and suffering get our attention. Shows that shock rack up massive viewership. Social media posts that provoke fear get readers.

I'd never dream of telling another human being what they should or should not consume from *any* of these sources, but I am absolutely certain that we all need to be *deliberate* about it. Because over time, the television commentator who keeps telling you to disdain another group of people based on who they voted for assumes a role in your story. Maybe the social media feed completely dedicated to denigrating people who've been caught on film during the worst moment of their lives takes one, too.

The question is: How much negativity are you going to let in? Which voices are you going to allow to whisper in your ear? Whenever possible, choose who you cast as information providers in your life just as carefully as you choose your in-real-life people.

The rest belong in the most distant circle you've got.

QUESTIONS
TO CONSIDER

> Are you actively choosing the people you cast in your circles? Too often we simply accept proximity for fate, not giving much thought to which relationships serve us, our families, our careers, our companies, and the greater good. The upshot? Unless you make a point of taking a bird's-eye view of the people who populate your life's story, they're just another thing that happens *to* you rather than a factor you thoughtfully consider.

> Are you respecting the sanctity of your sacred circle? Is there someone in this circle who deserves more of your time and attention? If so, how can you make that happen? (Hint: Look at your calendar. If they're not on it, make a change today.)

> Are you cultivating a Betterment Circle? Is it populated with a cast of characters who deserve your respect and emulation? Are you ensuring you're giving as much benefit to this group as you take?

> If you are in a position of power, are you supporting your people in their circles? Do you create metrics that are tied to results rather than time chained to a desk? Do you acknowledge that *sick* means *too sick to work* and mean it? Do you respect the fact that every person on your team has their own sacred circle? Or that they need a betterment circle to support them?

▪ CANNONBALL BOOK CLUB FAVORITE ▪

You're Not Listening: What You're Missing and Why It Matters

Kate Murphy

CHAD'S NOTE: As entertaining as it is informational, this great book breaks down our modern crisis of connection by looking at how we communicate with one another and how we can do it better. It's got healthy doses of history, neuroscience, and psychology, and they all come together to create a title that will make you feel smarter, more sensitive, and more capable of building great relationships by the time you close the cover. An amazing tool for anyone focused on casting their circles, and an especially timely read in our age of cancel culture.

Anyone who has shared something personal and received a thoughtless or uncomprehending response knows how it makes your soul want to crawl back in its hiding place.

Whether someone is confessing a misdeed, proposing an idea, sharing a dream, revealing an anxiety, or recalling a significant event—that person is giving up a piece of him or herself.

And if you don't handle it with care, the person will start to edit future conversations with you, knowing, "I can't be real with this person."

9

CULTIVATE CANNONBALL MOMENTS

What's the payoff of your story?

Are you relishing this ride?

When we tell a story or listen to one, we're tuned in for certain universal, basic elements—a theme, a plotline, stakes to make us care, a voice we can connect with and get to know, structure we can follow, and characters who grow and change. But where does it all lead? At the end of the day, we're looking for what publishers call the *payoff*.

There are countless forms it can take: the big reveal at the end of a mystery. The moment the lovers finally get together in a romance. The day the good guy takes his sweet revenge on the bad guy in a drama. The revelation that changes your mind or calls you to action in thought-provoking nonfiction. And in almost any genre, the moment when pieces fall into place and you think: *Wow. We were heading here all this time!*

The best stories don't have just a single payoff. They keep them coming. In a chapter here, at the end of a page there, gathering all the threads together at the end.

Stories without continual payoffs just invite indifference.

Your life's story—all your life's stories—are no different. They are worthy of great payoff moments. And just like in any other kind of storytelling, sometimes you have to work to make them happen and bring them to light.

When I founded my coaching company, I named it Cannonball Moments. When I started my podcast, I named it *The Cannonball Mindset*. I have a thing about cannonballs, because in my life's stories they represent the payoffs. Here's why:

———

The year my family put in our pool, we decided to throw a late-August party. We invited more than twenty families. We set a start time in the early afternoon, but we left it open-ended, figuring it would probably wrap itself up soon after dark.

What took shape that day was the quintessential end-of-summer bash. The weather was perfect. The pool was warm. The adults ate and drank, swam and talked and picked crab (because, you know, Maryland). The kids played tag in the yard and Marco Polo in the pool, and they splashed each other and every adult they could possibly reach. They ran in and out, in and out of the house, leaving a trail of pool toys and wet towels and Popsicle sticks in their wake.

We were having such a good time that the whole thing made a seamless transition from day to night. By 10 PM, the kids had made their way inside to watch TV, play cards, and settle in on the couches. My girls, who were nine years old that summer, changed into their pajamas—the universal sign that a child's day is done.

As things were winding down for the adults, I stood beside the pool chatting with a friend. I was facing the water, and his back was to it. I said something—I have no recollection of what—and this guy just turned around, fully clothed, and cannonballed into the pool.

The splash radius had to be fifteen feet, and I waited for him to wipe his eyes and look up before asking, "What the hell are you doing?"

All he said was, "I don't know—sometimes you just feel the need to cannonball."

I laughed, muttered, "You're an idiot," and started to walk away. But I only got a few steps. The idea was in my head, and it was pretty damned tempting. So instead of picking up dirty plates, hanging up the wet towels on the pool deck, or just starting up another conversation, I turned around, took off at a run, and did my own cannonball—bettering my friend's splash radius by at least a couple feet.

And just like that, there were two idiots in the pool.

My wife was in the house, watching this unfold through a window. Now, she has a more reserved personality than mine. She's thoughtful. She takes her time with things. So I was open-mouth shocked when I saw her running—through the kitchen, across the family room, onto the deck, down the stairs, and finally, with mischief in her eyes and a huge grin on her face, across the deck and—in one great leap—into the pool. Cannonball!

This is a woman who surprises and delights me all the time, but *that* was an epic moment. And as soon as it happened, a whole different level of party was underway.

People started leaping into the water from all sides—all these adults who'd stayed poolside most of the day were running and jumping and squealing like little kids. Which of course roused the actual kids from the corners of the house where they'd curled up for some quiet time.

My daughters came running to investigate the noise, careened out onto the deck, and slammed on the brakes. For a minute they just stood there, mouths open, trying to process the scene.

And then they were like, "Dad???"

It was written all over their faces that they wanted *in* on this.

What else could I say but *"Go ahead! Just go for it!"*

These girls do everything together—and so they backed up, side by side, to get a running start. Then they took off in tandem, rapidly closing the ten feet between them and the edge of the pool. And then they jumped.

That instant, when their mom and I were in the pool and these amazing children who own my heart came soaring out over the water, I looked up at them and caught their eyes and saw nothing but love and joy and happiness and everything that's right with the world.

That moment, that image, is burned into my brain. It is the antithesis of my old Little League photo and everything it meant to me. It's the antidote. To this day, I can close my eyes and picture my girls jumping. I can feel that joy as if I'm right in that moment again. And I swear, if that's the last memory I carry with me when I leave this earth, it'll be a gift.

I'd had cannonball moments before, but I didn't have a name for them until that night.

This was a moment when I knew, 100 percent, that everything I'd ever done or felt or suffered in my life had been worth it. It was a moment when my purpose and my path forward were clear. That feeling. That connection. That community. That joy. I thought, *This is what I'm here for. This is the story I'm going to tell.*

Of course, there was no winding down the party after that. It was cannonball after cannonball and all the kids back in the pool and all those families having a blast until the last guests packed it in just shy of two in the morning.

When I went upstairs to tuck the girls into bed, they were groggy and happy after such a long, fun day. I kissed them each goodnight and had one foot out the bedroom door when Mackenzie whispered, "Dad??"

"What, honey?"

"That was the best day of our life."

For a father, it doesn't get any better than that. Another cannonball moment.

Downstairs, Kim and I surveyed the mess, then stood side by side at the kitchen sink as I told her what Mackenzie said. I told her that sixteen years after we first made our vows to each other, I was ready to make another one. It seemed like the easiest thing in the world to say, "I am going to spend the rest of my life trying to create cannonball moments—for you, for the girls, and for everyone else who crosses my path."

I've really never looked back. This is what my life's about now. Every time I get to coach. Every time I get to speak. Every time I visit my daughters at college. Every time I swim in that pool or sit down to dinner with my wife. I'm always looking for and creating and appreciating my cannonball moments.

That's the story of my fascination with all things cannonball. And those are the payoffs in my life's stories. What's missing, of course—what it took me some time to figure out—was just how I could share it. It's one thing to have those moments for yourself, but it's even more satisfying to help someone else experience and appreciate their transformative power.

CULTIVATING A CANNONBALL-FILLED LIFE

I recently did an exercise with a group where I asked them to think back on the entirety of their past year and write down all the cannonball moments they'd experienced. In that room, we talked a little about what does and doesn't make the cut. If you cultivated it, created it, or played an active role, it's a cannonball moment. If it happened on the news and you were just a distant observer (even if it made an indelible impression on you), it's not. A cannonball moment might be a big event like a wedding or a concert, but it can equally be a small one like a sunrise hike or going fishing with your kid. It can be a joyful moment or one that's bittersweet. And it should always be, on some level, a source of fulfillment. Getting to have one last conversation with a dying grandparent, for example, is an entirely different kind of cannonball moment from dancing on the beach in Hawaii, but each is indelible and consequential. Each is a moment that becomes woven into the fabric of your superhero cape—that layer of love and grace and assurance and individuality that you're always either adding to or pulling threads from.

Each participant in my group accepted a blank sheet of paper and a pen. A few started writing immediately. Others stared at their pages for a long while. I put five minutes on the clock. At the end of it, each person had written down what they could remember, what they knew they'd cultivated and created that was worthy of putting on the list.

Now, I've done this exercise thousands of times over the last few years, so I had some idea of what to expect. But in each new room, you can always hear a pin drop after we count up the cannonball moments and share the average number.

Because it's seven.

Out of 365 days, the average person can identify *seven* of them that stuck. That are worthy of remembering.

You could argue that this is because people were put on the spot or didn't have time to think, but this isn't an especially structured exercise. People had their phones; some had their calendars; they had enough time to give it some thought.

And still, most found so few moments worthy of the *cannonball* label that their pages remained largely blank.

Getting to have one last conversation with a dying grandparent, for example, is an entirely different kind of cannonball moment from dancing on the beach in Hawaii, but each is indelible and consequential. Each is a moment that becomes woven into the fabric of your superhero cape—that layer of love and grace and assurance and individuality that you're always either adding to or pulling threads from.

Let's do just a little math on this. My friend Jesse Itzler, an amazing entrepreneur and author, walked me through this formula years ago—and my perception of passing time has never been the same.

The average life expectancy in the United States is seventy-seven. Let's say you're fifty—right in that sweet spot where you've established yourself in your career, maybe grown a family, maybe had the privilege of becoming a mentor or a leader. You've seen a lot of life; you have a lot of life ahead. If you live to that average age, you've got twenty-seven years left (though I hope you will have many more).

If that's the total years left in your life, and we stick to the average number of moments, then how many memorable, magical cannonball moments do you have left?

Answer: 189.

Happy with that?

If you're like me—if you're like most people I do this exercise with—the answer isn't just *no*; it's *hell no!*

It's *I don't want to talk to you anymore today, Chad.*

I've even had a couple *Don't you dare try to tell me . . .* exchanges come up. Because when you tell someone it looks like they've got nearly three decades to live and only about half a year of it will be worth remembering, it doesn't sit well.

And why would it? We all want to believe our lives are richer and more fulfilling and more rewarding than that. I mean, we should at least be having one cannonball a week, right? Or maybe a cannonball a day? We deserve better than seven highlights on a year's reel.

Here's the thing: If those numbers don't add up for you, then it is *up to you* to cultivate a different record. One with more moments. Better memories.

In order to do that, I urge you to try one or all of these four things:

1: Seek. Look for your cannonball moments. Expect them. Create them. Roll out of bed in the morning thinking about the cannonball moments that may lie ahead, about how you can lay the groundwork for them, and about how you can be present and engaged when they happen. Maybe that means steering a passing conversation into a deeper one, in which you express how much you care. Maybe it means you take the time to make your partner or your kids laugh out loud before you head to work in the morning. Maybe it means you put your phone in a drawer, get outside, and let yourself be dazzled with a little natural beauty. Maybe you pay someone an unexpected compliment or commit a simple act of kindness.

The moments are there to be had. Some are already happening and you just need to notice. Some are latent opportunities for you to add the cannonball magic to them.

When those moments happen? *Stop* for a beat. *Feel* gratitude. And then take it one more step:

2: Document. Dictate your cannonball moments as a memo on your phone. Or write them in a journal. Or take a minute to send yourself an email every day with the best of the day's moments. Even better? Take a picture. Remember back in chapter 1 when I mentioned I had 67,262 photos in my phone? Now, three months later, I have 541 more. Documenting my cannonball moments is the single biggest reason I'm obsessed with taking so many photos. They're a vibrant, immediate, rich record of my life. They're one of the big reasons that if you give me a blank sheet of paper and a pen and ask me for a list of the best and brightest days of my last year in a five-minute window, I'm going to need more time, more paper, and maybe even more ink.

3: Revisit. The more you remember, the more you remember. Make sense? Here's how: Experiencing a moment puts it in your memory, but most of your memories fall to the subconscious wayside after a short period of time. Maybe in an hour, or a day, or a week. Our minds are designed to be most focused on what's happening now rather than on what's happened in the past. Documenting a memory will help you retain it—help you make it part of the collage of your treasured experiences. Going back and reading about or looking at that memory later will take your mind and your senses back to the moment—help you stay connected to it.

So read the journal. Open the memos or the emails. Look at the photographs. Do it as often as you can. Your time investment is negligible, but your return on it is nothing less than an infusion of gratitude, purpose, and peace.

My own practice is this: Every morning at 5 AM, I look at my photos from that same date in previous years. On the day I'm writing this, those memories include a flight from Maryland to Montana (and a breathtaking view from the wide-open blue sky the state is famous for) at the one-year mark. A business trip to Louisiana that let me catch up with an old friend while taking a run together at the two-year mark. A golf game at a country club in Calusa Pines, Florida, with a coaching client and friend at the three-year mark. An amazing visit to my sister and my niece in Texas at the six-year mark. Attending my daughters' swim meet and cheering them on at the eight-year mark. Going out to a fabulous dinner with my wife and two of our closest friends at the nine-year mark.

And all the way back at the fourteen-year mark? Wrangling my twin four-year-old daughters in the back seat of our car in a Kirkland's parking lot, getting them giggling so hard I thought somebody might wet their pants, thinking, *What we're building here, this family, is the best thing that's ever come into my life.*

Every day, I revisit a stack of cannonball moments (some of them from before I'd even dubbed them "cannonball"), and I recommit them into my Memory Hall of Fame. It is such an easy, effective, and fulfilling part of my day that I am constantly advising my coaching clients to try it: *Take more pictures! You can thank me later!*

4: Share. This is probably the most important step I take every morning as I cultivate a life full of cannonball moments. That photo of the big Montana sky? That was just for me—a moment of quiet beauty at the outset of a crazy busy day. But most of my cannonball moments from this date were shared with other people, and every morning I make a point to share them back.

To my friend who went running with me in Louisiana, I texted the selfie we took together with a note that said, *Two years ago we had this epic run, my friend. Thanks for the cannonball moment.*

To my golf buddy in Calusa Pines, I sent a picture and a note: *Hard to believe it's been three years since we teed this up. Amazing day. Thanks for the cannonball moment.*

I reached out to my sister, to my niece. I sent my girls a picture from their swim meet, when they were still gangly pre-teens just beginning to discover what strong, capable athletes they could be. And another from that day in the parking lot, when my cannonball moment came down to just pinching myself that I am lucky enough to be their dad.

I called my wife and reminded her of our date. *Remember that night? Great food, great friends? I'm so grateful for all of my cannonball moments with you.*

And when I came across a photo from a year when this day was *not* a great day, when I was struggling, I memorialized that, too. I took the time to acknowledge: *This is where you were. Look at how far you've come.* Often, those less than great memories provide me with an opportunity to reach out and thank someone who led me or pushed me or said something encouraging or funny or kind that helped me move through a tough time.

The fact is, we are all hardwired for connection, and our connections are best and strongest when we experience them together, remember them together, and celebrate them together. It only takes a minute to do this for someone who shared a cannonball moment with you.

———

As I write this, I've started the last 2,403 days of my life with this practice. It takes just a few minutes of my morning, every morning—and it continues to be one of the most impactful ways I know to deepen ties with people in each of my circles.

BEARING WITNESS

Here's a counterintuitive truth: There are times when the best thing you can do to help another person to a cannonball moment is taking one giant step back. You can choose to bear witness.

So often, it's people with big, bold personalities who find their way to leadership positions. The ability to take a bull by the horns, get things done, and create big moments is an unqualified asset. But there are countless other ways things get done. If you're a bull wrangler, remember that the people in our circles—whether they're family, friends, colleagues, mentees, or employees—tend to grow into the space they're given and the faith we put in them.

When the baseball player you've coached for a year steps up to the plate and hits his first clutch home run, that's not your hit or your win, and not *quite* your cannonball moment. But it is magic all the same; it will fuel you to keep coaching and keep hoping.

When the intern who's shadowed your team for three months, taking tons of notes but rarely saying a word, writes an A-plus thesis about your work, that's not your paper or your grade, and not *quite* your cannonball moment. But it'll for sure inspire you to keep mentoring young talent.

When the sales exec you unquestioningly supported while she worked through a period of illness and absenteeism comes back into the fray and announces she's landed an account that'll bring in the biggest commission of her life, that's not your sale or your immediate payday, and not *quite* your cannonball moment. But it'll make you feel ten feet tall all the same—because you're genuinely happy for her, and because you waited with full faith.

If you're a business owner, manager, parent, coach, or mentor, I bet you've experienced another person's cannonball moment with this level of connection and satisfaction—and I bet it's within your power to foster more.

As a culture, we talk a lot about letting people learn from their mistakes, but we should be at least as quick to want to see them shine in their successes.

I hadn't thought a whole lot about "ownership" of cannonball moments until the year my daughter Mackenzie volunteered to raise money for the Leukemia & Lymphoma Society. Mac's always been quick to jump into new experiences—throwing herself into learning to surf, distance running, starting a podcast, volunteering at an animal shelter, and other adventures. She did each with the minimum of fanfare—simply following her interests to see where they might lead.

In fact, the whole animal shelter thing came as a total surprise to me. We sent our girls off to college, and within a few weeks I started seeing social media posts where Mackenzie was taking dogs I'd never even heard of for long drives in her car, walks in parks, and even out for ice cream. She was narrating these posts with information about each dog's on-leash manners, likes and dislikes, exercise needs, and personality quirks. All because, she informed me when I finally asked what the heck was going on, personalizing the dogs helps them get adopted.

It was because of this side of Mac's personality that I was unsurprised when she decided to join the leukemia and lymphoma drive—and also unsurprised when she didn't volunteer a whole lot of information about how it was going. And then one night, as we sat at dinner talking about our days, she nonchalantly mentioned that she'd blown by her $5,000 goal and decided to double it.

I set down my fork and stared. That's a lot of money for a seventeen-year-old to quietly raise in small donations.

I wondered just how big a deal I should make out of this, because the one thing that was crystal clear was that this effort wasn't yet completed. Mackenzie wasn't celebrating. She wasn't hanging up her clipboard and donation sheets. And she wasn't asking for my help.

She was just quietly eating her dinner and chatting about school.

A small voice in my head said *not yet*. It's a voice I've heard before—one I've too often chosen to ignore. As parents, as employers and managers, as leaders, we've all heard this one—a staying force when what we want to do is dive in and help (or take over). I try to be especially mindful of this because, well, I take up a lot of space. I'm a big person with big energy. I'm never under the radar, and it's far too easy for me to step on other people's toes.

I've had to learn when it's time for me to take a step back instead of a leap forward. I was pretty sure this was one of those times.

Two weeks later as we gathered for another meal, Mac made another low-key announcement: Her total had hit $10,000, and she was going to keep going. This dinner was different, though, because since we'd first talked about the fundraiser, she'd thrown herself into learning about blood cancers. She'd deepened her care and her commitment, because, she said, she wanted to be credible when she asked for contributions.

With that in mind, Mackenzie decided to go big. She was going to pursue corporate donations. After that, day after day, she was on the phone asking for appointments, sometimes with the heads of billion-dollar companies. She prepped a PowerPoint presentation. She gathered facts and stats and used each meeting to help her get a bigger meeting. In what seemed like the blink of an eye, her undertaking grew from the story of a high schooler knocking on doors for small cash donations to one of a young woman marching into corporate boardrooms and asking for seriously big checks.

As a family, we stood ready to help, but this was her party. Aside from asking me to run the 5K she was organizing and serve as the test audience for her fundraising presentation, she was firmly independent, quietly courageous, and utterly determined.

Her new goal was $20,000. Then $40,000. Then $50,000 . . .

In the end, Mackenzie raised $60,000 for her cause—one of the biggest totals in our state, and enough to secure her place at the Leukemia & Lymphoma Society's end-of-year gala. Our family would attend as her guests.

The events of those few weeks are how it happened that I ended up standing near a long reception line, watching strangers come up, one by one, to shake hands with my seventeen-year-old daughter and say *thank you* for her hard work and contribution. Mackenzie took it all in stride, but she was lit up from within. This was a cannonball moment that would forever be part of her story.

The night was not my accomplishment; it wasn't *my* big moment. And yet it was one of the great privileges of my life to watch the evening unfold. To bear witness.

QUESTIONS
TO CONSIDER

> How can you create cannonball moments for others? How many cannonball moments can you create for your family? For your colleagues? For your customers? One of my favorite things about my work is that not a day goes by when I don't receive a text from someone I've worked with in a coaching capacity because they want to share a cannonball moment. If it was the only perk of the job, I'd keep showing up every day.

> Do the cannonball moments keep coming? It's easy to misinterpret the desire to have cannonball moments as just another goal to set and achieve. If that's your initial reaction, I'd ask you to reconsider. There is no endgame or finish line in this premise. It's a practice worthy of enjoying and engaging every day.

> How can you make lemonade? Many of our less-brilliant, beginning-of-the-climb moments can become cannonball worthy when we set them alongside what happened next— whether that was a day later or a decade down the line. They become the basis of some of the best stories we tell ourselves—the ones in which we persevered or conquered or understood.

> Want to go one step further? Your cannonball moments are the foundations of the stories that shape your legacy. Share them with your children. Make them part of your story. Invite your family to make cannonball moments with you. They will become a beautiful part of your shared story.

• CANNONBALL BOOK CLUB FAVORITE •

The Power of Moments: Why Certain Experiences
Have Extraordinary Impact

Chip Heath and Dan Heath

CHAD'S NOTE: Whether you're looking to cultivate and recognize cannonball moments in your own life or facilitate them for someone else, the Heath brothers' fascinating, heavily researched book helps you understand what kinds of experiences stick in your mind and which are quickly forgotten. It's an equally outstanding resource for anyone who feels stuck in a rut and for anyone who seeks to make a true impact in the lives of others.

> *This is the great trap of life: One day rolls into the next, and a year goes by, and we still haven't had that conversation we always meant to have. Still haven't created that peak moment . . . Still haven't seen the northern lights.*
>
> *We walk a flatland that could have been a mountain range.*

10

KEEP TELLING: STORIES THAT STICK

We're always building our legacy.

How do you make people feel? How are you growing? What do you contribute?

It's impossible to conclude any conversation about the things you keep telling yourself without considering how those same statements and stories land with everyone else. What do your spouse and kids, friends and colleagues take away from the things you say and the stories you believe? In many ways, the answer to that question is at the center of how you partner, how you mentor, and how you lead.

We all know the feeling of closing a book and having it "stick"—having the ideas, the characters, or the voice resonate so powerfully that they stay with us for hours, days, or even the rest of our lives.

That phenomenon doesn't just happen when the stories and statements are in ink or between two covers. It happens every day in every one of our lives. We call it *legacy*. And while many people don't give it much consideration until reaching the end of life, we can choose to take stock every day—considering our impact, working to grow and to give.

ENDGAME: ONE WAY TO MAKE A LASTING IMPRESSION

There's an oft-repeated legend that when the brother of Alfred Nobel, the inventor of dynamite, died, a French newspaper mistakenly published an obituary for Al. The year was 1888, and the headline declared "The Merchant of Death is Dead."

Nobel was appalled. Was this really going to be the sum of his life?

He'd patented his big invention (one of hundreds) with many industrial applications in mind. Mining, construction of canals and tunnels, railroad expansion—they were all made easier and more affordable with dynamite. But you can't control what people do with your ideas once you turn them loose—so Nobel became one of the richest men of his time and watched this particular invention help tear worlds apart in nineteenth-century wars.

The "Merchant of Death" headline would have rattled anyone, would have gotten just about any living soul to stop and think about their legacy. It certainly seems Nobel took the charge to heart, because eight years later when he did die, instead of leaving the bulk of his wealth (over $200 million in today's dollars) to his extended family, he left instructions for that money to establish awards for achievement in the sciences and the arts.

More than a century later, the Nobel prizes remain among our most important recognitions of excellence and contribution. And the best known of those awards—the Nobel Peace Prize—may be the most prestigious honor in the world.

The upshot? Alfred Nobel didn't just manage to eke out a win after the gruesome headline that cast him as a warmonger (which was not entirely untrue, but that's a different story); he managed to rewrite his story in a way that would forever link his name to the concept of *peace*. His bequest may have been the single most effective rebranding campaign of all time.

That's one way to do it—to write your most enduring story in a postscript to your life—but the truth is, for most people legacy doesn't come down to the final flourish of a pen (or a massive bequest). Nobel's saga is the life's work equivalent of writing a three-act play, and then coming out during the encore and throwing gold coins to the audience. It's not the plot of the story, not the characters, not the acting that the crowd will likely remember. It's not even whether they loved or hated the show. It's the razzle-dazzle at the end.

And that would all be well and good if it weren't for the fact that Alfred Nobel was, by his own account and those of many others, a lonely and unhappy man through most of his life.

IS TODAY A GOOD DAY?

Which brings us to that other way of looking at legacy, one acknowledging that the enduring parts of our stories don't just happen at the end. Nor do they typically end up with our names on them.

Instead, our stories that stick are woven into our days, accomplishments, and relationships. We share them every day—as partners, parents, leaders, innovators, and contributors. Cannonball moments, for example, are legacy moments—marked and memorialized for a short while or a lifetime. They're one aspect of your story that endures.

But what about the rest? There are thousands, maybe millions, of important moments in every life that go unsung but nevertheless have an impact.

I believe most of those—most of the moments that define whether your day's efforts or your life's work resonate with any other human being—come down to three essential threads woven throughout your stories: *connection, growth,* and *contribution.*

Any time you want to check in on how you're leading, on the impact you're making, on how your legacy is shaping up, you need only ask the corresponding questions:

> *How do you make people feel?*
> *How are you growing?*
> *What do you contribute?*

Those don't sound like end-of-life questions to me. They sound worthy of asking every day. Because legacy questions aren't just about whether anybody will remember you or anything you did; they're the most immediate and relevant way to check up on the stories we keep telling ourselves. Every person I know who's experienced great growth and betterment in their adult life started out by raising their level of awareness—by asking these or similar questions of themselves and moving away from old assumptions on a regular basis.

In my own life, I've taken this one step further to help me stay mindful of this biggest-picture perspective. Every morning, it's as much a part of my routine as brushing my teeth to ask those three questions about connection, growth, and contribution.

And then I ask one more: *Is today a good day to die?*

I don't have a death wish. (In fact, I fully intend to live past a hundred.) I have a wish to live well. I have a wish to have an impact. I have a wish to leave the people I love with blessings from their time with me instead of burdens. The good-day-to-die question frames my day in terms of what I've done, what I need to do, and the status of my relationships. It makes me consider my unfinished business. And it sets me on the path to a day lived in line with my values.

Is it extreme? Maybe a little—but I spent far too many years wasting time, wasting energy, and focusing on all the ways the world was unfair. I squandered a lot, and I am done with that. In that context, taking each day as a new invitation to assess how I'm doing, who I'm reaching, and whether I'm contributing? That's just common sense.

Most of the moments that define whether your day's efforts or your life's work resonate with any other human being come down to three essential threads woven throughout your stories: connection, growth, and contribution.

HOW DO YOU MAKE PEOPLE FEEL?

Are your words and your energy drawing people in, or are they pushing them away?

I came into the real estate industry at a time when even long-timers were running away as if the houses were actually on fire.

As luck would have it, I didn't yet know enough about home sales to even notice what was happening, let alone wonder if maybe I should be running, too. And despite a worldwide downturn in the field, I found success.

The reason? I was arguably the corniest salesman in the history of the industry. I looked at every person who entered my orbit not in terms of their value as a sales prospect but in terms of the moments I wanted them to have in their new homes. I could picture those lives like I was seeing a slideshow of the future: how they'd live their love stories, play with their dogs, raise their children, host holiday celebrations, and even sit side by side on the porch and grow old together. My mentality was Hallmark all the way. In truth, long before I defined the beautiful everyday moments of my own life as *cannonball moments* and started cataloging them for my story, I was dreaming them up for everyone I met. My enthusiasm was genuine enough to be contagious—and that combination translated into sales.

And so while every stat tied to the real estate industry was in free fall, I was keeping track of construction timetables, hosting showings and final walk-throughs, sitting in at closings, handing over keys and bottles of champagne and teary-eyed congratulations. I was doing it so often that for four consecutive years, I was among the top new-homes salespeople in the nation.

The secret to that success wasn't in any method or technique, not in any gimmick I used to seal a deal or get anybody over the finish line. It was in the simple fact that people *know* when you care about them. We feel the positive energy of genuine connection.

Putting focus on people over processes, positions, corporate goals, and individual achievements brings only good to your professional life. And as a coach, I've had the opportunity to see the guiding principle of seeking connection change team dynamics, change management/employee relations, boost sales, revolutionize hiring practices, and help countless people feel better about how they spend their days. Best of all, time and time again I meet with corporate clients who tell me they are taking these principles home—applying them in their marriages, in their parenting, and in their friendships.

When I first started coaching, I was shocked at how often a lack of respectful, mutual connection was at the root of a problem—not just in nearly every business and personnel problem, but equally in families and peer relationships. I adopted *Coach the person, not the position* as a mantra, and that helped. But even then, sometimes I had to be blunt. There's one conversation I have with every CEO, every head of personnel, every boss, and every employee who's struggling to make things work—especially those who aspire to be achievers and leaders. It starts like this:

Every person on your team has a reason they get out of bed in the morning. Do you know what it is?

As I was writing these pages, I came across an article about "quiet quitting"—and was genuinely surprised to see how widely it's attributed to economic and geographic factors like pay packages, remote work, and the perks a company does or does not offer. While all those issues may play a role, I firmly believe the root of this movement comes down to people disregarding the fundamental responsibility we have to treat each other with respect and caring. Quiet quitters do not feel recognized. Most of them have not felt recognized for a long time—long enough for them to give up trying to earn what they need. So they slump down at their desks, and they do the minimum, and they bide their time until they find some new opportunity that makes them feel hopeful again. This happens with the lowest-paid employees—absolutely. But it happens with the highest paid as well. Because at the end of the day there is simply no substitute for respect and recognition.

This doesn't just happen in offices. It also happens in our homes. If you don't invest the time and energy to let your spouse, your kids, your parents, your siblings know how much you respect and value and care for them, they'll quiet quit on you, too. And that's a whole different level of trouble and pain.

> *Quiet quitters do not feel recognized. Most of them have not felt recognized for a long time—long enough for them to give up trying to earn what they need.*
>
> *So they slump down at their desks, and they do the minimum, and they bide their time until they find some new opportunity that makes them feel hopeful again.*

If you want to be able to answer the question of how you make people feel with something positive, start by incorporating respect and affection into communications across your sphere of influence.

Look, you can get a ton of mileage and goodwill out of a simple "Good morning! How are you today?" You can demonstrate your respect by taking an "I see you. I hear you. You matter" approach to every interaction. But when you're ready to do better? Ask questions. To connect? Ask questions. To show respect? Ask questions. To empower? Ask questions. Not "How's your Friday?" or "Is that report about ready?" but questions that celebrate behaviors. Pick something someone is doing right and notice. Ask how. Ask what that person had to overcome. Say, "Tell me more."

I've gotten pushback from a handful of executives who worry asking about process will somehow imply they don't know their field, but that's just not true. Most of the smartest people you'll encounter in this world won't be giving answers. They'll be asking questions. They'll want to know more.

When you do this with authentic interest and caring, you change the game. You create connection. You build memories. You inspire success.

I can tell you from experience, after giving ten thousand talks around the globe, that no matter the metrics, no matter the growth, no matter what anybody says at the end of a seminar or a conference, I know that my greatest professional achievements come in the moments when someone who felt unseen, felt unheard, felt unworthy experiences a SHIFT to being seen, being heard, and feeling worthy.

We all need to be mindful that nobody is going to remember how many houses we built or cars we sold. Nobody will remember how many employees we had or how many square feet were in our homes. There will be no data on our tombstones except the dates we were born and died. But in the short term and the long, even after your exact words disappear on the wind, even after the memory of your face starts to blur, people will remember how you made them feel.

Make it a mission to make them feel appreciated, empowered, capable, and worthy. The stories of how you made that happen are the ones that will stick.

> *In the short term and the long, even after your exact words*
> *disappear on the wind, even after the memory of your face starts*
> *to blur, people will remember how you made them feel.*

NEXT-LEVEL CONNECTION? COLLABORATION

As a parent or spouse, employee or employer, I'm willing to bet you see moments every day when the people you love or work with get bogged down by their shit and can't seem to pull themselves out. It's painful to witness and frustrating to share—especially if you're invested in that person's success or happiness.

We all know you can't fix other people's problems. But can you help? Over years of observing how excellent leaders work with their teams, one behavior has stuck with me over any other—and that's a willingness to collaborate for a greater good. The idea that you might look at my problems and say, "Oh, I see this is important to you. Let's roll up our sleeves and see if we can make a dent in it together," shows a commitment beyond any words. And the fact of the matter is that when you see an opportunity to spur an action, you may just help your employee or coworker or child or spouse get over the first hurdle to a solution—or to betterment.

People are always looking for a monumental change, but all change happens in incremental steps. So offer to walk alongside, to set up the training—even just to sit down and talk it out. Do it with no agenda except lending a hand and being a source of empowerment.

In my own work, I frequently meet with clients who are unhappy about their health. It's a concern that weighs on their relationships, on their confidence, and sometimes even on their job performance. Over the years, I've gone on at least a thousand runs in a hundred cities with individuals in my coaching groups. We run that first mile, or two, or three. We commiserate about how hard the first day can be. We talk about life and love, work and family. We witness sunrises and storms, stifling heat and bitter cold, quiet paths and congested sidewalks. Friendships are born. Legs are cramped.

I would be hard-pressed to say whether I'm the one who gets more out of those mornings or whether it's my companions—but I know that quite a few of those runs were the first of many for my clients, and that sometimes they were the first steps on journeys back to health.

The truth is, you can't take anyone else's journey for them. You have to respect their right to choose and walk their path. But that shouldn't stop you from saying: "Need any help?" or "I'd love to do that with you" or "I've got half an hour right now."

At its best, this is an exercise in helping another human being start to rewrite a story of their own. At its most basic, it's another way to be mindful of how you make people feel. We all need a collaborator or a coconspirator from time to time. If you take your opportunities to fill that role, you'll be writing stories that stick.

HOW ARE YOU GROWING? DO YOU MAKE GREAT MISTAKES?

As I write this, one of the new experiments I've added to my routine is taping my mouth shut before bed each night. I read about the downsides of mouth breathing—that it can lead to sleep disorders and that your lungs function less optimally with cold air coming in through the mouth than with air warmed on its way through your nose—and I thought changing my sleep habit would be a great step toward peak health. I don't know if it's going to work. I just know I'm going to try.

When my wife came to bed the first night of this and saw the big strip of black tape across my mouth, she said, startled, "*What is going on?*"

So I pulled the tape off (just as unpleasant as it sounds) and explained.

Kim looked at me, a little amused, a little confused, and always okay with me going my own way, and said, "Every day it's something new with you. When's it gonna end?"

I said, "Probably when I die," kissed her goodnight, re-taped my mouth, and drifted off to sleep. I am lucky enough to have a family and a big extended tribe of people who completely get the need I feel to do this kind of stuff. They may joke sometimes, but they don't judge, and they never ask me to stop.

I jump into new things to a large extent for myself, because I love to experiment and learn. But I also do it for my daughters, for my employees, for my coaching clients, and yes, even for my wife who has to put up with it. Because at the end of the day, I'm committed to creating an environment that tells everyone around me: *If you want to try something, big or small, ultimately successful or not, go for it.*

I want them to feel safe.

I believe that as a leader—in the office and equally in your home—you're not building your greatest legacy unless you can create an environment where the people around you know it's okay to fail.

Sara Blakely, the founder of Spanx and one of the few self-made female billionaires in the country, has said that when she was growing up, every night at dinner her father would ask each member of the family, "What did you fail at today?"

As a teenager, Blakely probably didn't much appreciate the question. But when she was building a business empire from the ground up, you can bet it helped propel her past one failure and rejection after another.

I've done this for a long time with the people in my own life, and it recently came back to me in the most poignant way I could imagine. One of my employees, who's a friend of our family, just became a father for the first time, and my eighteen-year-old daughter called him and asked if she could offer a bit of parenting advice. I imagine he braced himself for what advice a teenager might have to share, but he told me later he intends to take her words to heart.

She said, "Create an environment where it's okay to do crazy things, to try anything new. My parents always did this—always supported us; always let us try. They let us succeed, and they let us fail."

Hearing about that call was a proud moment for me as a dad. Because I have seen just how deep the fear of failing can run and how crippling it can be. Nobody wants to feel disappointment. Nobody wants to feel shame. But if you "protect" the people around you from feeling those emotions, then you stifle them from learning how to overcome them and move forward. You may even deter them from learning to be resilient—which may be the most critical life skill of all.

Sometimes your people are going to have crazy, big ideas. They're going to get inspired. And it's really easy for us to fall into the habit of tamping that down—often without even thinking about it. But it's the crazy-idea people who become our biggest success stories. They push limits. They think big. They get acquainted with their genius. They fail, and they learn to keep going.

If you keep telling yourself that you want to be better, but you're not willing to fail, you're not creating half the legacy you could spin if you'd take a few chances and show everyone who looks up to you that it's okay for them to do so, too.

And by the way, when you do it, own it.

Whether you're going to eat vegan or write a book, create an app or take up golf, spend a sabbatical in a monastery or learn to surf—be unapologetic in owning your decision and every action that follows. Love it? Fantastic. Find it doesn't suit you? That's great, too, as long as you *choose* to stop and own that decision. *I'm out* is a perfectly acceptable statement. *I can't because* is less so. You don't owe it to anybody in this world to follow through on your new hobby or career or journey of self-exploration. But you owe it to yourself and everyone who is part of your story to be clear that *you* are the cause and effect of your own successes and failures.

When you own both the mundane and the crazy shit that happens in your life, you show everyone in your orbit what it looks like when a person is fully accountable for their choices and actions. And that is just as much a part of your legacy—of your story that sticks—as making big moves in the first place.

Dr. Edith Eger, one of my biggest heroes, wrote that "the ultimate key to freedom is to keep becoming who you truly are." I believe the way we do this is to roll up our sleeves, try new things, and own both our behaviors and our actions.

When you own both the mundane and the crazy shit that happens in your life, you show everyone in your orbit what it looks like when a person is fully accountable for their choices and actions. And that is just as much a part of your legacy—of your story that sticks—as making big moves in the first place.

WHAT DO YOU CONTRIBUTE?

At the end of every interview episode of *The Cannonball Mindset* podcast, I ask the same question, and it's this: *Fifty or sixty years from now, what do you want your contribution to have been?*

I've had one main driving intention at my company and in my life for the past ten years—and that is nothing less than to contribute to the well-being of every human being I interact with. It's my mission statement. I've got it framed on the wall. Ask any Cannonball employee and they will tell you that's at the core of what we do.

We don't do it for profit. We don't do it for ego. We don't do it because it's a good look. We do not, like George Costanza in the famous *Seinfeld* episode, only put something in the tip jar when the world is watching. We contribute on as many levels as we can because of a fundamental trust that this is what we're here for, and that the more we contribute, the better our lives get.

Philosophers and innovators, leaders and teachers have been telling us this for ages. The ancient Roman philosopher Seneca wrote: "Wherever there is a human being, there is an opportunity for kindness." Dickens wrote: "No one is useless in this world who lightens the burdens of another." And Eleanor Roosevelt, master of the memorable one-liner, said, "When you cease to make a contribution, you begin to die."

There is magic in finding ways to take a little of your time, money, knowledge, or goodwill and give it away. Pay a compliment. Make a donation. Teach something. Tip generously. See a need and go ahead and meet it. Acts of contribution that take two minutes of your time are just as worthwhile as the ones you work at all your life. They all become part of your story, part of your self-view.

Sometimes that has to be enough, because as you go through your days honoring a commitment to contribute, you can't always know what will go unnoticed, what will be appreciated, what will make a difference. Sometimes your contribution isn't met with open arms. Sometimes it'll sit around for days or months or years—and *then* become of use.

And so all you can do is give freely and often. Plant the seed of a story that empowers a friend. Lay a pickaxe for breaking through self-limiting assumptions at your employee's feet. You can't make them pick it up. You can't make them swing it. You may *know* they could use it to chip away at the stories and beliefs that are holding them back, but the giving is your contribution.

I recently had an experience in home maintenance that seemed a perfect example of how this works. I can't share this without confessing: I am not a handy person. I stink at all things manual labor. But if you look in my garage, you'll find a ton of tools, because in my physical life, just like in my emotional life, I like to be prepared. So when my wife asked me to clean the vent over our kitchen range, I thought, *I can handle that.* I unscrewed the thing, then immediately lost my grip and let it drop behind our giant stove. Even though I have ridiculously long arms, I couldn't reach it. So I grabbed the oven by the door, gave it a tug to move the whole thing away from the wall, and pulled the door clear off.

At that point, I was grumbling—*you've gotta be kidding me.* I tried to climb behind this stove on my hands and knees. I tried to crawl over the counter. I couldn't figure out how to get it back to rights.

And then it hit me: *I have the tool for this!*

I remembered that on one of my trips to Home Depot (where I do like to *buy* tools), I'd gotten a mechanical arm gadget. I found it in the garage, reached it behind the stove, and pulled the vent right out. From there I was able to rinse it off, reinstall it, and put the oven door back on (seriously, who knew pulling on the door is how it's designed to come apart?).

That *I have the tool for this!* feeling is such a great emotion. It is incredibly satisfying to look at a problem—no matter how serious, simple, or complex—and have your mind confidently recognize that you can handle it. And what I have realized more and more in recent years is that we are each imparted with the life equivalent of an unfillable toolbox. Call it a gift from God or call it biological destiny, but we are *always* learning. And if we choose to grow and better ourselves, then we can use that learning to stock our box with the critical tools of a life well lived. Tools to deal with hard feelings, to analyze complex problems, to soothe rushes of anger or adrenaline, to practice patience.

How many of the tools in your toolbox came courtesy of someone else's contribution? And how often did you recognize in the moment: *This is going to matter for me?* Half the time? A quarter of the time? Once in a while? All those skills, coping mechanisms, and insights that are in you are part of someone else's legacy—gifts that helped you learn. And every day that you freely give whatever knowledge and support and understanding you have to share, you're doing that for the people who are watching you.

You contribute what you have, then one day when that other person is in a pinch, when they're struggling, when they don't have a story to meet the moment, they may remember and use the tool you shared. If you've contributed tolerance, or resilience, or perseverance, or generosity, you can't possibly know if or when someone else is going to pick that up and make it their own—but you can give it, and you can hope.

> *We are each imparted with the life equivalent of an*
> *unfillable toolbox.*
>
> *Call it a gift from God or call it biological destiny, but we are*
> *always learning. And if we choose to grow and better ourselves,*
> *then we can use that learning to stock our box with the critical*
> *tools of a life well lived.*

NEXT-LEVEL CONTRIBUTION? FACILITATION

If you keep telling yourself it's your job to fix everyone who matters to you, to jump into their story and change everything, you'll never let them get comfortable with their own authority. Your job as a leader is not to commandeer another person's story. It's to help whoever's looking to you to see themselves in that role.

If you're asking them, "How are you the hero of this story?" you're on the right track.

A couple years ago I ran the Chicago Marathon with my daughter Madison. She was seventeen at the time—one of the youngest entrants in the event that year. That event goes down in the story of my life as one of my greatest days, but also as one of the most difficult.

We had trained for months. Madison doesn't do anything halfway, and this was no different. If she was going to run the race, she was going to be prepared, so we ran early mornings and late evenings, weekdays and weekends, in rain and in sunshine, together and apart.

By the time we lined up for the start of the race, my personal goal was a simple one: run side by side with my daughter. However her run went, mine would go the same. I'd run Chicago twice before, but the stakes that morning had nothing to do with me or my time or even whether I crossed the finish line.

At the five-mile mark, we were running in sync, feeling strong. Madison carried herself like a seasoned athlete—confident in the work she'd done to prepare. At ten miles, we were still on pace. At twelve, though, I could see she was starting to feel the strain. She got quiet and stayed focused, continuing to put one foot in front of the other, but I could see her grimacing with pain.

Fun fact: Marathons are painful for almost everyone. One University of Georgia study conducted in September 2021 polling over twelve hundred marathon runners reported that 99.8 percent of them experienced pain during the race. Eighty percent categorized their pain as "intense." As you pound out mile after mile, your thighs, hamstrings, and calves take a beating, and their nerves can become inflamed. Abdominal cramps are common. Many runners report chest pain, neck pain, and, of course, foot pain. That last one always seems to get me, and I have ten frequently bruised, bent, and sometimes nailless toes to prove it.

At the seventeen-mile mark, pain came for Madison, and she hit a wall. She was physically and emotionally spent, struggling for each breath, with tears streaming down. As she watched runners pass us by, I could almost see the stories she'd been telling herself about the day shift from tales of finishing strong to tales of giving up.

As a father, my first instinct was to tell her it was okay to quit. I knew I could make that easier for her. I could say, *You're obviously hurting. You're the youngest here. You've come* seventeen miles *and that's enough.*

But there was a part of me that knew it was not my place to step in and close the door on her race or her narrative of it. I wasn't there to motivate or push her to the end, but I wasn't there to cosign on her deciding she couldn't do it, either.

All I could do was facilitate her owning the story, whichever way she wanted it to go.

So I asked her, "Madison, remember that training run we did in the rain?"

She nodded but said nothing.

I said, "Remember how hard that day was? You were in so much pain."

"Yeah," she nodded again.

"What did you do?" I asked. "How'd you overcome it?"

"You remember, Dad," she said. "I just did it a little at a time. I said, 'I can make it up this hill,' and did it."

We pushed ahead a little further. She continued to struggle, but she was moving forward.

I asked about her hardest training run. About the day it was so hot we'd almost called it off—and probably should have. I asked how she'd prepared.

And even though she continued to struggle, I could see her changing the narrative—weaving in her previous successes and all the times she'd overcome tough conditions and exhaustion and discomfort.

Miles twenty through twenty-six were grueling, but my daughter's narrative kept her going. She stepped back into her role as the star of the story, and she pushed forward.

The route for the Chicago Marathon is largely flat, but as you approach the end, there's a big hill. When you come over it, you can see clear to the finish line—the last .2 stretch of the 26.2-mile run. When we came around that corner, I said, "Madison, this is all you."

Then I stopped and watched her run that last .2 miles as if it was her first. She ran it like a victor. When she raised her arms at the finish line, it took my breath away.

One of my all-time favorite photos—a snapshot that's burned into my brain—is the one the organizers of the marathon took of Madison crossing the line. She's facing the camera, her arms up, determination and relief and joy etched across her face. And if you look *way* back in the distance of that photo you can see me, too— standing still in the middle of the street, watching her reach the end, applauding.

The truth is, you can't run anyone else's race. You can't carry their burden. But you can ask questions. You can facilitate. You can ask them how they do great things and how they continue to grow and get better.

And sometimes, when you stand in the wings and do these things, you earn the opportunity to see another human being take a step into their own. This was one of those times. And if I can have even just a few of those moments in my life's legacy, I'll be satisfied.

> *The truth is, you can't run anyone else's race. You can't carry their burden. But you can ask questions. You can facilitate. You can ask them how they do great things and how they continue to grow and get better.*

QUESTIONS
TO CONSIDER

> How do you make people feel? Do they lean in to you? Do they pull away? When you make this assessment, start with the people who matter most to you. Helping them feel loved and safe and empowered is an essential piece of both your impact and your own fulfillment—a piece that spills over into every other area of your life.
> - Do you have someone who makes this hard? Most of us do. You can only control what you do and say. That's it. So give your goodwill. Choose kind words. Wish peace and prosperity. And then know you have done your part.
> How are you growing? I don't care how old you are or how much you've already accomplished, you have to be able to answer this question. What are you doing to learn? What are you doing to keep from getting stuck in a rut?

What are you trying that's new? What have you failed at lately?

> What is your contribution right now? What do you want it to be in the future? You don't have to start a foundation or build a monument to contribute to the greater good. When I answer this question, I always put raising two strong, powerful young women at the top of my list. I put using my stories as a starting point for growth. I put all those times I asked someone who was looking for a change to come for a walk or a run. What small contributions in your daily life are adding up to your legacy? What big contributions do you use to define yourself? What did you give freely today?

▪ CANNONBALL BOOK CLUB FAVORITES ▪

Living with a SEAL: 31 Days Training with the Toughest Man on the Planet

Jesse Itzler

CHAD'S NOTE: This book about a man who, on impulse, asks a former Navy SEAL to move into his home and be his personal trainer for thirty days was a kick in the pants for me. Who does that kind of thing? Itzler gave himself 110 percent to this experiment, basically getting his ass handed to him day after day by a man with a stony personality and brutal commitment of self-discipline. The book is funny (something most of my favorites are not) but, more importantly, it was a spark for me. If this author could willingly subject himself to sleep deprivation, punishing workouts, and almost constant discomfort for thirty days to get out of his rut, what could I do? (Spoiler alert: One of the first things was to reach out to invite Itzler on my podcast, because this was someone I wanted to better understand.)

When you think you're done, you're only at forty percent of what your body is capable of doing. That's just the limit we put on ourselves.

The Hard Parts: A Memoir of Courage and Triumph

Oksana Masters

CHAD'S NOTE: I read *The Hard Parts* as I was writing this book, and when I finished it I couldn't bring myself to shelve it. I kept it on my desk, picking it up again and again. I put this book right up there with Edith Eger's *The Choice*. It is a story of hardship and fierce will, of overcoming, of astronomical growth and depth. Masters's mighty achievements as an athlete are only equaled by the depth of her character. This is a top-ten-of-all-time book for me.

You are not the product of where you came from. You are not what happened to you.
Regardless of the taint of how you were treated, there's beauty in you.

EPILOGUE

The Twelve-Hour Think

In the fall of 2022, I signed up to participate in an endurance run called the JFK 50 Mile. I'd run an ultramarathon before, entering with a big group of friends who kept each other company start to finish. We cheered each other on, commiserated about our blisters, our aching muscles, and the cramps that came and went. Even during the stretches when we were too tired to talk, we enjoyed the comforts of being in a pack.

The JFK was different. I started with a small group, but many of those runners are regular ultramarathoners and I'm not—so by the fifth mile, when we'd each set our pace, I was comfortably near the back of the pack, focused on completing the race, not on competing with anyone else.

Because of the dangerous footing on long stretches of the course, this race has a strict policy banning runners from wearing listening devices—no headphones or earbuds, so no music or podcasts. I'd trained, studied the route, and psyched myself up for the grueling length of the day—but I had in no way prepared for spending *twelve hours* alone with my thoughts. I hadn't even considered what that might be like. I went into what was, by far, the longest stretch of waking hours I've spent without speaking to another person in decades, thinking more about my feet than my head.

Most of the first fifteen miles of the course is on the Appalachian Trail, along a rocky, dramatically scenic mountain ridge. During this stretch, I kept my focus on the placement of my feet. I ran to a rhythm of: *Don't slip. Don't stumble. DAMN it's cold. Don't slip. Don't stumble.*

At the 14.5-mile mark, I made my way down the steepest part of the route, a series of descending switchbacks that loses a thousand feet of altitude in a hurry. I took even greater care with every footfall until the terrain leveled out, and then I followed the course to the dirt-and-stone C&O Canal Towpath that runs along the Potomac River. The towpath portion of the race alone is more than a marathon's length, and it is completely flat, utterly quiet, and, by comparison to the grueling gauntlet and rugged beauty of the Appalachian Trail, a pretty boring run.

By mile twenty-five, the excitement and energy that had carried me to the halfway point began to fade, and my inner critic piped up. It started in about how cold I was; how hungry; how sore; how alone. I couldn't see any other runners, but I was well aware most of them were ahead of me—so far up I couldn't see a soul.

Although I knew better, I let the dark thoughts in anyway, a running commentary of doubt and derision: *Why am I doing this? I'm not physically or mentally fit for it. This is all a façade—I'm not a real runner. I'm not going to make it.*

I tried to turn it around, to appreciate the beauty of the river, to get psyched about how far I'd come. I've spent the last ten-plus years of my life learning how to handle those negative thoughts, how to put them in perspective, how to replace them with stories about my effort and growth and inner strength—and about the fact that there are people who love me.

But sometimes, just like anybody else, I get weak—and a marathon's worth of silence in tough conditions got into my head. I let the inner critic put me down, insult me, and make me feel unworthy.

At mile thirty-five, when a runner came up behind me, weaved around, and continued on past, I watched his back recede and was suddenly intensely mindful of the race's cutoff points—of how if I didn't make it to each in time I'd be pulled out of the field.

My feet kept moving, but now I was doing ultramarathon math in my head—trying to calculate my pace, the distance I'd traveled, the maximum timeline of the race, how far to the next cutoff point. I was also calculating just how much misery I'd feel if I'd come this far only to be sent home.

By mile thirty-nine, I'd convinced myself I wasn't going to make it. The critic got quiet—like this was already a KO, like all that was left was to wait for me to quit. I'd been running for eight-plus hours, and I had nothing left—no strength, no willpower.

At mile forty, another stranger came running up behind me. He didn't slow down or meet my eyes as I chugged along, still freaking out about that next cutoff and the humiliation that surely awaited me there. When the guy came even with me, he kept his gaze ahead, but he startled me by speaking. The sound cut through the silence I'd been living in all day, and it was as jarring to me as a shout through a bullhorn.

What he said was, "If you run ten-minute miles for the rest of this race, you make the cutoffs." He powered on before I could even respond. But in his wake I was like, *Wait! What?! I still have a SHOT??* I was starving, exhausted, sore, and freezing—but I *know* I can run a ten-minute mile. I've been beating that pace for five years, even when I'm tired, even when I'm uncomfortable, even when it's the last mile instead of the first.

And just like that I was *running* again.

Sometimes we forget that no matter what the world throws at us, the hardest thing to endure is the roller coaster of emotions that come along for the ride. Whether you're dealing with an inconvenience or a tragedy, you start telling yourself stories that hurt at your core—doom and gloom all the way.

This is the end of the world.

I can't survive.

I'm not worthy of being here.

I'll never be warm or comfortable or happy again.

And when it happens, the path of least resistance is to float along on all that misery for a while. That afternoon I was thinking I was *out,* and then a stranger came along with the smallest gesture of kindness and brought me back. He probably has no idea that he changed my day.

From then on, I was back on my game, and I had ten more miles of silence to reflect on everything that is good in my life, on every reason I have to keep going, on every story that makes me stronger.

I ran it like a catalog. I thought of my wife, of my girls, of my amazing team at Cannonball Moments, of my siblings, my mom, and my friends. I thought of the people who invite me to speak, and the coaching clients who bring such an incredible sense of purpose and collaboration to my life. The list got long, and I picked up my pace. As I hit the last mile, it was two experiences with coaching clients that bubbled up and took me to the finish.

The first happened years ago in Michigan. I'd been working with a corporate team for months when one of the executives brought her teenaged daughter to my training day. I was honored. I told my story and we talked about the power of our words and our fundamental, innate ability to grow and learn and get better. At the end of the day, I asked this high school freshman if she had one word to describe how she felt after her training day.

And she said *capable*.

Seven years passed between that day and the JFK race, but *capable* stuck. I've kept in touch with that girl—now a woman with a college degree and a career. She still tells me she feels capable, and that she's never forgotten that day.

That memory kept me running.

The second story happened more recently, at a talk in Texas. I always bring a box of Brené Brown–inspired bracelets to my events that say *I AM ENOUGH*. In the years since a friend first gave me one, I've never been without one myself, and I hand them out to every single new client as a foundation of the work we're about to do. My own bracelet has become an invaluable talisman for me (believe me—you'll never find me without it). When the story in my head goes dark, when I start to feel broken, it snaps me back to center. I'm a visual learner. I need to see it. And that day on the C&O Towpath, I somehow forgot it was there under the cuff of my sleeve—until the mile-forty runner broke my silence.

After that Texas talk, the company's human resources rep asked if I had any bracelets left. She wanted to take one home to her son.

The next day she came looking for me.

"I gave him the bracelet," she said.

"Great. Do you think he'll want to wear it?"

And she said, "I think so, but something else happened."

I asked her to tell me more, and she explained that after she gave this teenager the bracelet, he said "thanks" and started to leave the room. As he walked away, she asked, "By the way, do you believe that? That you're enough?"

He said, "Yeah, sure."

But a minute later, with one foot out the door, he stopped and said, "Except that I'm a senior in high school and I don't know where I'm going to college.

"Except that I'm not sure I can pass AP Bio.

"Except that I've never had a girlfriend."

The HR rep's eyes welled as she told the story, and then she said, "We've never had a conversation like that before. It opened a door I didn't even know was there."

That story kicked my run into a higher gear—to hell with the hunger and the cold and the toenail I could feel coming loose inside my shoe.

One thing I know for sure: Excitement and energy could not carry me over fifty miles. Training could not take me fifty miles. Discipline couldn't do it either. But those memories, those stories, those pieces of my own personal Superman cape—they allowed me to power across the finish line. To go home proud and happy.

———

My best and last advice is this:

Be the author of your life. Pick up the pen and embrace the task.

Decide which stories define you, what roles you play, what energy you exude, and who you welcome into your circles.

Structure your days, weeks, and years to align with what you love and who you want to be.

Choose to cultivate and share cannonball moments, stringing them like so many streetlights and stars along the timeline of your life.

Give the people around you the courtesy of being seen, heard, and valued.

Strive to become the masterwork you were born to be.

Keep telling yourself stories of connection, growth, and contribution. Keep telling yourself you are worthy and capable and strong.

Your words and your stories will help carry you anyplace you want to go.

ABOUT THE AUTHOR

CHAD SANSCHAGRIN
Entrepreneur, CEO, Author,
International Keynote Speaker, Coach

Chad Sanschagrin is a dynamic entrepreneur dedicated to empowering others to realize their full potential. As an influential executive, leadership, and sales coach, Chad inspires and motivates through his impactful keynote presentations and transformative coaching.

Chad is the founder of Cannonball Moments, a leadership and sales coaching company that provides consistent training to teams across various industries. The mission of Cannonball Moments is to enhance the well-being of individuals by helping them achieve their potential, fostering a life enriched with love, health, success, and joy. Chad's effective strategies help executives and teams develop a growth mindset, resulting in increased sales conversions and personal fulfillment.

In addition to his coaching endeavors, Chad hosts *The Cannonball Mindset* podcast, where he amplifies the voices of other influential leaders. Notable guests have included Gary Vaynerchuk, Jesse Itzler, and Shawn Nelson.

Outside of his professional life, Chad is an accomplished Ironman and marathon runner. He enjoys a fulfilling family life with his wife and their twin daughters.